With Those Who Grieve

WITH
THOSE
WHO
GRIEVE

Kay Soder-Alderfer

LION
PUBLISHING

Copyright © 1994 Kay Soder-Alderfer

Published by
Lion Publishing
20 Lincoln Avenue, Elgin, IL 60120, USA
ISBN 0 7459 2624 X

First edition 1994

All rights reserved. Except for brief excerpts for review purposes, no part of this book may be reproduced or used in any form without prior written permission from the publisher.

Cover design by Paetzold Design
Interior design by Bob Dienethal
Edited by Robert Bittner

CIP applied for

Printed and bound in the USA

To my parents
who gave me life
and taught me to love it.
To David
who has helped me celebrate life.
To Sylvia and Nancy
who helped me find courage to live again.
To Lisa, Sara, and Tom
who have brought color to my life.
And to God
who has laughed and cried with me
through it all.

My views of death and grieving have been formed in part by three brave pioneers. Twenty years ago I trained briefly with a marvelous woman, Dr. Elisabeth Kübler-Ross. Her observations and listening to dying patients helped her formulate five stages known by many in the grieving process: denial and isolation, anger, bargaining, depression, and acceptance.

I am grateful to Dr. Kübler-Ross for her pioneering work. And while some people have only heard of the five stages she posited, she said many times that grief wasn't that tidy. Above all else, I believe she held up a beacon to a subject that had been previously taboo in our society: death and its accompanying grief.

Reverend Granger Westberg, author of *Good Grief,* is the second pioneer who has had an influence on me. His work in viewing persons and systems holistically started years ago. From him and others I have learned the importance of working with the whole person—physically, emotionally, psychologically, and spiritually—throughout the grieving process.

The third pioneer is the late Dr. Virginia Satir. First, as a student in workshops, and later as she advised me on research, Dr. Satir was professional, compassionate, and genuine. I still miss her greatly.

The people who have taught me best about grief are all of the people who have entrusted their stories to me—for this book, and for years before this book took shape. They, too, have been, and are, pioneers in the land of grief.

Preface

A book never writes itself. Believe me, there are times I gladly would have allowed my word processor to take off on its own and produce a beautiful manuscript. But day after day, I came back and found the screen waiting. Still empty.

Grief is a lot like that. Suddenly, we are visited with news of the death of a loved one, and we face it without a script. It's a blank page, waiting. Empty.

When we hear someone has died—that they have been in an accident, that they have killed themselves, that a medical mishap has occurred, that natural causes or a terminal illness as painful as AIDS or cancer has finally ended a life—we are handed a book. The news of their death is on the cover, but the rest of the book is blank, waiting for the grief process to unfold.

Grief does unfold. Feeling upon feeling, thought upon thought, surprise upon surprise, day after day. We move from the initial shock and sadness into a variety of feelings. They visit us in the night, and we can't make sense of them in the morning.

This book is about courage. Through their courage, people bravely told me their stories of grief. Sometimes through tears, sometimes stoically, sometimes needing to take a few months' respite between interviews because the pain was too great. But they had stories they were willing to tell. In part to "write" some of their own grief process. In part to help others who are grieving. My own response is one of humility to all who were willing to speak honestly of their experiences.

It also took courage to publish this book. What seemed a simple assignment bumped up against incredible odds to see this book in print. So, my heartfelt thanks to my editor, Bob Bittner, and to all at Lion Publishing who believed in the worth of this project and made it a reality. My thanks to Claire Buettner for her research skills and compassion.

My thanks to God, who had the heart and wisdom to provide me with parents who affirm all of life, and who have helped me to trust in the potential for goodness in every day and every person. I thank my family and friends who have supported me throughout my struggles with this work and throughout my life as I've embraced life, death, and so much in between.

Peggy, thank you for showing me so much of life and teaching me I could somehow survive your death. To all who have loved me and allowed me to love them so that both their lives and deaths mattered, thank you. To the two Swedes in a pod, Sue Crowfoot, my Deaconess Sisters, Sister Nancy, Joan Barth, and Lily Wu, my thanks for helping me, at least from time to time, to know the true peace that passes understanding.

Contents

Foreword

I met Peggy when I was a freshman in high school. She loved music, good books, good times, and challenges. We never realized the challenge we would face four years later.

The summer after we graduated, I went camping out West for most of the summer. Peggy had been out East attending college on a terrific scholarship. During our phone calls we talked about how great it would be to see each other again.

When I returned from my vacation, our reunion was in a local hospital. Peggy had inoperable cancer. Our visits were few. Within weeks, I received a phone call that Peggy was dead. That was the first time I felt the tentacles of grief take hold of me. Part of me would never again be quite the same.

Five years later I was the one attending school out East. In my first year of seminary, a very dear and intelligent professor spent hours listening to me recount my confusion, my sadness that returned uninvited, my grief story of a close friend's death. "I don't understand why she had to die so young when she had all that promise," I blurted out to him one day. He looked at me kindly and said simply, "Do you understand there are some things we will never understand?" That was the beginning of my becoming unstuck from my grief. Two years later—twenty years ago—I worked as a parish educator and counselor; death and grief counseling were woven into my daily work.

I never meant to remain in grief work, but whether I was a teacher, journalist, therapist, spiritual director or administrator, my job path somehow kept intersecting with people who grieve. About ten years ago, I understood better why: I have a natural bent toward healing, wholeness, and life. If I attracted people desiring the same, I was going to attract people who mourned—precisely because they, too, value life so much.

Throughout much of my life, I have been a wounded healer. In a society that values image and perfection, the concept of a wounded healer is not enthusiastically embraced. But I find the reason some people are such a good match with me is that they, too, acknowledge their woundedness and ache to find wholeness again. One of our most devastating wounds is the death of someone we love or with whom we wish we had had a more loving relationship.

When I was contacted to write this book, I was working as a therapist, a spiritual director, and a journalist. Since I worked with or wrote about grief frequently, I honestly had hoped for a happier topic. But while grief wouldn't have been the topic of first choice for me, I agreed to write it knowing clients and others were seeking help with their grief.

I assumed that I could approach this book on strictly a professional level. Since I have listened to more than 500 people tell their grief stories, I figured what would be a few more? Even though I have been touched deeply by nearly 100 deaths, I wasn't ready for the journey of this book. I honestly think I was operating with some incredible notion that death and grief would not touch me personally while I wrote.

How wrong I was! First I encountered a life-threatening illness during which I had to reconsider seriously my priorities. Shortly after signing the contract, I found out my cousin, Sue, had a return of her cancer. My lifetime mentor developed leukemia and is now living beyond the prognosis given her. One of my spiritual directors died. My father, always in robust health, underwent two heart procedures and two cancer operations within four months.

Funerals are more frequent occurrences now as I enter midlife. Friends are losing parents, children, spouses.

As I interviewed some people, I realized we had similar losses. Some interviews were more difficult than others, not only for the people being interviewed, but because of the pain those people's stories would touch in me. Other interviews were scheduled and rescheduled until finally someone would courageously admit, "I'm not ready yet."

In the midst of everything that made me question if I could ever complete this book, three things happened that gave me the hope and determination to continue. The first was a young client who was having behavioral problems in school because of unresolved grief. One day he smiled at me and said, "I like coming to see you 'cause you listen with your heart."

His comment triggered my second reason for continuing. I need hope to live fully, and I became aware that I need only a thimbleful of hope to continue. In my work, I believe no healing happens without God's presence and hope. This became more and more obvious as I myself needed to feel that healing presence in my own life. I discovered I had enough hope to get through what I thought I'd never have the strength to survive.

Third, when I had spent several visits interviewing one person, I finally realized why I wanted to write this book. I wanted to let others know of the humanity, genuineness, power, and hopefulness of listening to each other's stories of grief.

This was my own written reflection at that moment:

> . . . I had now been brought into Char's life in an ineffable way. There is something in the telling of stories of loss that somehow binds us together in sadness, hope, healing, and, for me, an intimacy beyond comprehension. The dynamics are both wrenching and profoundly touching. All pretense is stripped away. Maybe it is one of the few ways we are truly, wonderfully human together. We grope for meaning in meaningless death, and somehow find a new shared life. This

is why, despite tears and sadness, I feel compelled
to do grief work. It is why I tell people I have the
best job in the world.

We have each other. We have our stories. And we must tell
them, even if we don't know why. For in the telling is the healing.
In the listening is the healing. Tell your stories from your heart.
Cry. Yell. Moan. Laugh. But, tell your stories.

And, please, listen with your heart to the stories of those
brave enough to honor you with their stories. Linger together.
For together, with God's help, we can heal from grief's agony.
Even if we must accept that there are simply some things we will
never understand.

Chapter One

Pioneers in the Land of Grief

No one can tell you how to grieve, though plenty of people will try. Some will tell you that you have grieved too long, or haven't grieved enough. Some will encourage you to express feelings you don't feel. Others may discourage you from expressing what you do feel.

Despite the fact that I have grieved many times, and that each grieving process has been different, I still cannot write out a prescription for healing that is sure to work in every situation. There isn't one.

When a grieving person or family comes to me, each road is different. Sometimes I feel like I am going up a mountain with someone; other times it is like a walk along the shoreline, including high and low tides. And I have had my share of feeling like I've gone along with a machete through some grief jungles.

However, after twenty years of grieving and of doing grief work, I have found a few similarities for many of us who grieve the loss of a loved one.

First, grieving is hard work. Grief may deplete you of energy you took for granted or challenge everything that you held dear or certain. This facet of grief will be discussed more in the following chapter.

It is essential that you take time to make sure you are in the best health possible. Getting proper rest, eating healthfully, and exercising are no luxury. They are some of the crucial ways you can maintain stamina to go on living. Perhaps you have heard of or know of someone who died within a fairly short period of time after losing a loved one. Grief can, in fact, be life threatening.

Second, no one "knows just how you feel." Your loss is yours. Your reaction is yours. The stories contained in this book are interviews with a variety of people who have grieved in a number of ways. You may identify with one person's reactions to grief, but not another's. Some situations will be closer to yours, but your reactions to your situation will be yours alone.

You had a special bond with someone. That person—and that relationship—cannot be replaced. Never again will you feel that person's touch; spontaneously laugh or talk together; be aggravated by, teased by, tenderly moved by, confused by, understood by that person in just that same way.

As grief is lived through, you will likely have memories of that person, many of which you may cherish the remainder of your life. While memories can be wonderful companions, they remain only memories. And memories cannot keep us warm at night in bed, be spontaneous, or hug and kiss us.

Third, people will say many things to you that seem insensitive, stupid, or ill-timed. Those remarks may fuel anger or hurt. You may feel lonely, and wonder why people say such things.

Pioneers in the Land of Grief

Some of us say such things not intending to harm or hurt another person, but out of our own needs. We want to be comforted and to comfort. In trying to comfort, our words too often come from a place inside us that doesn't want to see you hurt. We believe that if we say something—anything—it will help you not hurt so much. Rarely do such words help.

Some of us also say awkward things because we haven't ourselves felt grief, or we haven't worked through our own grief, or we haven't come to terms with our own mortality. If a friend or other support person seems unable to find ways to support you during this painful time, you may want to have her read chapter three on grief etiquette, or consider writing down things you would find helpful and distribute copies of your list to friends and other support people. Many people find it a big help to know what kind of support you would like. Grieving is complicated enough without losing friends and other potential supporters.

Fourth, grief is a healing process. Like any wound, you need and deserve time to heal from the loss you have experienced. We all heal differently and at different rates. Be gentle with yourself. Grief is an enormous wound—it often becomes like a systemic condition, at least for a while. Allow yourself the time that you need to grieve so that you can move on.

Because grief is a process, many people are surprised that they suddenly break out crying after they thought they had cried all the tears possible. Someone may gesture with their hands, walk with a particular gait, speak in a voice that suddenly triggers renewed feelings of missing the one who has died.

Other people say that they are surprised how grief seemed to "suddenly disappear" from their lives. After so many days that seemed to point to the contrary, once again they feel alive. They have more pleasant days than unpleasant ones. They have more energy. They have said their good-bye. They are ready now to say their hello to life again, knowing it will be different and full of changes, including future losses.

In some cases, people never get over grieving a death. This seems to be especially true for people who have lost children. It is also often true for those who have lost someone through a violent or sudden event, such as an auto accident or violent crime. It can be true for anyone.

After helping people for twenty years to face and survive grief, I am frequently asked, "How can I get through this?" or, "What have you found that helps you get over grief?"

Being with those who grieve, I know that there are a few things that seem to help many people. Support is important for many people. Those who have family or friends to offer needed support usually have an easier time with grief. Not necessarily an easy trip, but an easier journey. Some people find their support in extended families or through groups designed to help people facing similar losses through the grief process. Some find help through counselors and clergy.

Those who have grief support remark frequently that it was necessary not only to talk through their grief with others but to know they were listened to. Many cherish those who would simply "be there" with them, with or without words. People who have grieved before do not necessarily have an "edge" over those who are facing a significant death for the first time, for each loss is unique. In fact, I have worked with people who become very impatient with themselves because they remember "the last time didn't take this long." But if they have truly gone through the grief process before, they do know that grief gets less painful over time. They know healing happens.

People who are accepting of their own mortality generally have a somewhat easier time in facing death. This doesn't mean that if you have accepted your mortality you won't hurt or ache or face the very real pain of death and grief. It does mean that you likely will see death—and life—with a different perspective. I have watched some people have a heightened awareness of life because death has forced them to come to grips with their own mortality.

Having a belief system, beyond counting on humanity to accomplish everything, helps many people through grief. Organized religion comforts some, but it is not a bulletproof vest against pain, nor against questioning cherished religious beliefs.

In fact, many people blame God for a death, and ask, "How could a loving God do this?" Others discover a spiritual sense for the first time in their lives when confronted with death, or they deepen their faith by finding a deeper meaning to life.

I encourage grieving people to yell at God or ask questions of God. This can be very difficult for some people. But I am always shown hope by these people. Their underlying assumption is that there is a God large enough to take our questions and complaints. After all, puny gods are of little help.

Despite what we may hear about near-death experiences, none of us really knows what form life after death might take. Some of us derive great comfort from believing death is not an ending, but a transition for our loved ones who have died. But that ignores one of the critical aspects of grief: you still face the void of that loss in this life. My answer to all who honor me by inviting me to walk their way through the grief process—and my answer as I face my own grief time and again—is that we must all answer the question, "How will I fill this void?"

This book is designed primarily to let those who grieve speak their truth. Through sharing the many stories of people who have known grief, it is my sincere desire that you will find hope, light, life, and love to help fill your void.

Chapter Two

If You Are Grieving

Whether you are grieving for the first time in your life, or are grieving for an uncountable number of times, each experience of grief is always different. Grief affects our whole being—physical, emotional, psychological, spiritual, and social. Our internal balance, our homeostasis is lost. We may well feel broken, and wonder if we will ever be whole again.

Perhaps some of the following descriptions of grief are close to your own experience. They are listed for two reasons. First, to offer possible comfort in knowing others have felt at least somewhat similarly as you. Second, to offer hope—for all of these quotes are from grief survivors, people who have gone through grief and now have again entered the mainstream of life.

"Grief is like a tornado that ripped out my very insides, leaving me to wonder if I could ever rebuild a life."

"When I went through grief, I felt I was on an emotional

roller coaster. No emotion seemed to last more than ten minutes, and then I was hit by another one."

"When I was at the bottom of my despair in grief, I wasn't sure that I could go on living. Getting out of bed was an effort. One day I found even breathing seemed to be an effort."

"When my husband was killed, at first I went into shock and just operated on automatic. Little by little, with God's help, I started to pilot my life again. But it meant a lot of test runs before I was ready to try flying again."

"I was OK until the casseroles didn't come anymore. As long as people told me what to do, I just did it. I asked no questions. But once I was really alone with my grief, the questions just kept coming and coming. The answers came much more slowly. I still don't have all the answers, but I do have hope back in my life. Hope can take you a very long way."

"I used to be afraid of volcanoes. Then my daughter killed herself, and a volcano seemed tiny in comparison to my anger."

"I was sure I believed in life after death until Juanita died. Then I seemed to wonder about everything I believed in."

"I thought I was through grieving. Jack had died two years before. I had cried and screamed and smashed a hole in the wall. Then a letter came addressed to Jack from an old army buddy, and I felt like I started to grieve all over again."

"Why does everybody make such a big deal out of grief? My mother died. She lived a full life. I handled the finances and other matters. I know she's happy in heaven. Why do people bother me by asking if I'm all right?"

"Of course I was sad my friend had died. I had known her since childhood. But I was so shocked by her death it seemed like all I could cry were 'dry tears.' It was three years before I really cried over her death, and once I started, I was afraid the tears would never stop."

"We had talked a lot about what we would do if one or the other of us died. I was all right with the paperwork and other details—in fact, they kept me busy. But then I seemed lost, nearly swallowed up by a huge, gray fog. I wished for a while that I had died instead."

"Grief, for me, was like a shadow always following me around . . . or like a piece of chewing gum that hung on and on to not only my sole, but my soul as well. I thought that I would be through grieving the day I had all the answers to death and dying. "Why her, God? Why now? Why me?" It took me a long time, but I finally realized that healing my grief no longer had so much to do with death and answers, but facing life and finding new questions."

"After six months, I decided I had grieved enough. During the next year I could not sleep well, I got headaches, I developed back trouble. My doctor ran test after test. She finally sat down with me and asked if I had taken time to grieve. I told her I grieved for six months, and that was long enough. She said, 'But your body is still grieving.' "

"At first, I was afraid to start enjoying myself again. I was afraid I would lose all memory of Tim. But little by little, I pushed myself back into life. I still had memories; they just didn't hurt so much."

"I knew I needed help the day a friend asked me how I was feeling. I told her I felt like I ate razor blades every day."

"I am richer for grieving. It's just a heck of a way to enrich your life."

"My grief never seemed to leave. Then I realized I had made

a sort of friend, or at least a companion, with grief. It took me a long time to realize that I would rather have the sadness of grief than risk loving again."

"I was convinced I would never feel happy again. I was wrong. When laughter was as natural as tears, I knew I would heal."

Perhaps one or more of these grief survivors' comments comes close to something you are feeling now. Or something that you felt yesterday, or will feel tomorrow. Perhaps your experience with death and grief has been or will be completely different.

The Physical Effects of Grief

Following are some examples of how profoundly and completely grief can affect us. Grief, like all of us who experience it, cannot be compartmentalized. But many grieving people experience the interplay of symptoms on the physical, mental, emotional, spiritual, and social levels.

> loss of appetite
> inability to sleep
> sleeping most of the time
> irregular sleeping patterns
> anorexia
> weight gain
> frequent headaches
> stomachaches
> chest pain
> blurred or changed vision
> lack of sex drive

occasional numbness in limbs, hands, or feet
menstrual difficulties
difficulties in breathing or swallowing
skin eruptions
bed wetting
fatigue
loss of physical balance
ringing in the ears
addiction to drugs and/or alcohol
onset of, or exacerbation of, serious illnesses

Grief itself is not an illness; it is a serious condition that affects us deeply. But if we deny our grief, or if grief takes over our lives, we can indeed become very ill.

The Mental Effects of Grief

One of the most frightening changes for some people occurs in their intellectual functioning. People frequently feel they are going crazy from grief. That thought or feeling is very real, but it will pass with time. Some other mental changes people have experienced include:

difficulty concentrating
forgetfulness
difficulty or inability to perform routine tasks
memory loss
nightmares
easily distracted
driven by only one thought or similar thoughts

suicidal or depressive thoughts
excessive daydreaming
mild to overwhelming confusion
losing or misplacing objects
missing appointments, celebration dates,
    even job interviews
distortions in perception
"seeing" the deceased in a crowd, only to learn it is
    someone else
distorted sense of time

The Emotional Effects of Grief

The emotional aspects of grief are perhaps the most poignant or powerful aspects many people are aware of. The following list includes some of the words people have used to describe their feelings at different times in their grieving process.

numb	hurt	shattered
hopeful	abandoned	failure
angry	shock	hopeless
guilt	rage	hollow
ambivalent	relieved	stressed
blame	helpless	dread
lonely	afraid	longing
shame	sadness	doubt
peace	despair	denial
empty	overwhelmed	paralyzed

I recently showed this list to a woman who had been grieving for nearly two years. She looked at me and said, "Yes, and I used to feel almost all of those in one day." Another person said, "No wonder I'm tired!"

No wonder indeed! Depending on your situation and temperament, and how you face grief, your feelings will vary from day to day and in intensity. Grief intensifies almost any feeling. But people who have survived grief report that their feelings lessen in magnitude as time passes. While you are deep in grief, you may think your feelings have *you*. As you heal, you realize *you* have your feelings.

The Social Effects of Grief

Some of us grieve in private; some in public; some in both. Friends may become concerned you are not doing the social things you used to do. While grieving, it is very likely that you will not feel like doing the same social things. One of the transforming powers of grief for some people is that as acceptance and hope appear, they realize the potential, in both a scary and exciting way, for living a whole new life.

Social changes can include:

> isolation
> avoiding places that hold fond memories of the one
> > who has died
> wanting to spend time only in such places
> being left out of activities you did as a couple,
> > with friends, or as a family
> too many well-intentioned invitations
> no or few invitations
> new friends, new opportunities

refusal to make new friends or to try new things,
    to avoid the risk of feeling another loss
workaholism
becoming too busy as a way of avoiding grief
clinging to familiar social patterns and customs
refusing to celebrate anything familiar because of
    the anticipated pain of being reminded of your loss

You will never again be quite the same person as you were before the death of a loved one. For some people, this means few changes. For others it may mean seeking companionship in a pet or person, traveling, moving, changing or starting work, making new living arrangements, or any of a myriad of other changes.

The Spiritual Effects of Grief

I am convinced that one of the most neglected and most important aspects of grief is how we are spiritually challenged and changed. For most people, grief is a time of immense spiritual questioning, changing, and often growth.

Spiritually, grief may mean we:

look at and accept our own mortality
wonder about cherished beliefs
question previously held beliefs
find meaning in God that we never had before
feel abandoned or punished by God
ask piercing questions like: "Why would a loving God let
    this happen to me?"
turn away from God

find comfort in our beliefs
become more reflective about spiritual matters
stay angry with God
express anger and all feelings to God, feeling a source
    of strength in that
find comfort in prayer and/or Scripture
feel we can find no comfort in prayer or Scripture
examine our own lives and how we wish to spend
    the remainder of them

Throughout our spiritual pilgrimage while grieving, we are likely to go down many different paths. No matter how many pathways I have traveled, each new grief brings me face to face again with feelings of spiritual poverty. Yet each time I also find great spiritual wealth awaiting me when I can rely on God to help me through. That is where I have found my sustaining hope, time and time again.

How Much Grief Is Too Much?

When my husband and I bought our first home, the previous owners had a feature we hadn't considered when making a decision whether or not to buy the home—a trash compactor.

It turned out to be an amazing feature. Each week our entire disposable garbage could be compacted into one tight, neat package about one square foot in size. Early in my ecological awareness days, I could almost sanctimoniously take the small package to the curb, feeling we had done our bit for the environment. What I did not realize was that garbage, compacted or not, was still garbage.

Nearly ten years later, on the brink of midlife, I had overworked and overcared to the point of near burnout: a dear friend was moving; I suffered a painful emotional trauma; I had moved, lost my job due to a merger, experienced migraines, and lost three people close to me.

I needed to balance myself, and one way I did that was to find both a spiritual director and a counselor.

I remember being startled by the clarity of my words when the counselor asked me what I needed help with: "I have compacted grief." We both worked diligently to help me peel away layers, not only of my own grief, but of pain I had taken on being a grief counselor. I wept. I got angry. I examined my reasons for wanting to continue with those who grieve. I discovered ways I could do that more effectively without taking on the pain of others. Then I grieved—for my losses and for the pain of so many others' losses.

It took nearly two years before I began to feel a "clearing place" inside. And then I thought of that old trash compactor. Perhaps the garbage had a sleek new shape, but it was still garbage. My internal "old trash" was grief, hidden in muscles as well as my mental and spiritual dwelling places. Grief is grief. And compacted grief is grief delayed, or denied.

Now, on the other side of the clearing-out process, I have deliberate ways of maintaining my physical, mental, emotional, social, and spiritual health daily. None of them can be ignored. That is, unless I want to spend time again cleaning out my grief compactor.

Finding Help
Through personal experience and the experiences of clients who

are grieving, these are some of the times and ways I suggest getting help.

1. While grieving, be sure to have at least an annual physical and check with your doctor if a physical symptom remains troublesome to you.

2. Avoid alcohol and drugs (some people need to avoid other behaviors such as overeating) while you are grieving. What begins as a way to alleviate pain can become habit shaping or even addictive. If such behaviors become habits, check with your physician, a counselor, or a 12-step or other recovery group.

3. Learn when you need to ask for support and when you need to go it alone. When asking for support from friends, family, and others, be as specific as possible. For instance, if you are feeling lonely, ask someone to go to a movie, to chat, to go for a walk or out with you for a meal, rather than saying, "I'm lonely," and expecting people to guess what you might need.

4. Get the specific support *you* need. Some people choose friends and family; some choose clergy or pastoral counselors; some choose professional counselors or other mental-health care workers; some choose spiritual directors or people who work primarily with grief; some choose support groups. I have found all of these sources helpful, depending on the grief situation and my reaction to the loss of the person who has died.

5. If trusted friends or family members suggest seeking professional help, ask them what they see in you that sparked their suggestion. Listen carefully. Often even a few sessions with a caring professional will help you decide if you need

such help or if you are "just" experiencing normal grief.

6. If you feel your grief has lasted too long, check with a professional trained in dealing with grief. Do the same if you are finding thoughts or feelings overwhelming, or cannot shake fatalistic thinking.

7. Consider joining a support group for persons who have experienced similar losses. Some places to check for grief support groups include local hospitals (many run 4-6 week groups), local churches, and local chapters of national organizations.

   To find such groups, check the phone book for social service agencies in your area, your local newspaper (if nothing appears in print, try calling the editor), your physician, a member of the clergy, or the social service or chaplaincy services of a hospital. Also, depending on your community, you may find a notice posted on a supermarket bulletin board or other public display areas. You may want to ask a trusted friend to attend a first meeting with you.

8. Some people find bibliotherapy (reading books and other materials for self-healing) very helpful. If you are a person who finds encouragement from reading, be sure to check with your local library for resources.

   Ask a research librarian to help you locate the materials you need. Most libraries, even in small communities, have interlibrary loans, which means you have access to books and other materials from several libraries besides your own. In addition, some libraries are capable of doing a "literature search" for you by computer of many resources related to grief in general, as well as specific concerns such as suicide, stillbirth, death of a child, and so on. If you live near a college library, many have a simple machine you can go to and scan or type in the topics you are interested in. There is often a small fee for this service.

9. If you or someone you know is familiar with computer bulletin boards, some help may be found through online support groups and other electronic resources.

10. Discover sources for hope that will get you through your grieving process. Perhaps listening to some music, expressing yourself artistically, going for a walk in the woods, jogging, or listening to nature helps you feel hopeful. Do what works best for you.

Chapter Three

Grief Etiquette: How to Offer Help to Those Who Grieve

In listening to grieving people, I have heard many say, "Isn't there some way to let people who want to help really *be* of help?" Many have searched for resources on "grief etiquette"— what is and is not helpful. Because you are an individual with your own life and death experiences, and every friend or relative will have a different set of experiences, it is impossible to say what is right for everyone in every situation.

For example, many people who have lost someone through a lingering illness began their grief process long before their loved one actually died. Others have been so busily involved in the minute-to-minute, day-in day-out care of the terminally ill that they have barely had time to begin to grieve. Despite attempts at public education, some who have lost loved ones to AIDS feel an additional burden of wanting to hide the cause of death and much of their grief.

Always take into account the person you are trying to comfort, as well as what you can do given who you are. Do not offer or promise support that you are not able to provide. Try not to be offended if someone turns down your offers to help. The person is not rejecting you or your ability to give; he or she is just saying, "I need to grieve in my own way—including the help I accept."

Despite the wide variety of situations of loss, many of the grieving people I have worked with have some concerns in common. A frequently voiced lament is, "Why do people say the things that they say?"

Listed below are some of the remarks most frequently found to be hurtful or insensitive. I have used actual client responses to explain why those comments are not helpful.

I know just how you feel.
> "How can someone know how *I* feel? Only those with a similar loss know"—Parent whose child died.

At least she isn't suffering anymore.
> "No, my wife isn't suffering anymore. But she isn't here to enjoy life, either. And now I am suffering the pain of being alone"—Max, whose wife died of cancer.

He really looks good (or real, or alive), doesn't he?
(At a visitation or viewing.)
> "Of course he doesn't look good or alive. He's dead. And

he *never* wore rouge!"—Millie, 82, commenting on the wake held for her husband.

I admire your strength. You've been an inspiration to me.

"Why do people assume I'm strong? That just puts one more expectation on me. Why can't people be inspired by my art or my other work? I don't want to be admired for surviving my sister's suicide"—Robin, age 27.

It must be wonderful to know that she is in heaven with God.

"If I hadn't hurt so much at the time, I would have said, 'Why, were you in heaven lately, and did you see her with God?' Maybe if I had said something, at least people would think before they speak"—Jacob, 47, six months after his wife was killed in an auto accident.

God must have had a reason.

"Even if God does have a reason for everything, I don't want to think about reasons right now. And why didn't more people say God had a reason for my boy's life as well as his death?"—Shirley, 52, two years after her adult son was killed.

You're young; you can have all the children you like.

"We had a dream. We made plans and prepared for our first child. We feel a deep pain. Maybe in time we'll want to try to have another baby. Right now we're getting over the shock of the stillbirth"—Linda and Ron, seven months after their first child was stillborn.

Why don't you ever cry?

> "People have no idea how much I cry, how deeply I hurt.
> I just need privacy right now"—Emily, 32, six weeks after
> her husband of two years died.

You've felt sorry for yourself long enough. Just snap out of it!

> "How long is long enough? I never expected to feel this
> sad for this long, but what I feel is grief, not self-pity"—
> Ted, 59, who lost his only child twelve years ago.

The best way I've found to get over grief is to help others.

> "I'm glad that my aunt found a way to get over her grief;
> it just won't work for me. I need my energy just for me
> and my family"—Janelle, 24, whose parents died in a
> freak accident.

These examples are not included to suggest that there is nothing we can say or do to help someone who is grieving. They are included to help all of us take the time to think before we speak, to use sensibility and sensitivity, especially soon after someone has died.

So, if none of these comments are helpful to those who grieve, what can we say or do that will help? Plenty! Though what people will find helpful or comforting varies according to temperament, experience, situation, and timing, there are some helps that many grieving people agree upon.

1. While people are grieving, accept that their moods may change drastically over short periods of time. Be patient

and don't expect them to "be their old selves." Even as grief begins to lift, they will never again be exactly the same person they were prior to a profound loss.

2. Don't think that you can "fix" the situation; none of us has that kind of power. But we can help by being ready to listen. If you want or need to say something, the most comforting words are simply, "I'm sorry," or "I'm with you if you need someone."

3. If you are a "doer," don't overdo. Ask people what would be most helpful. Or offer to do some concrete, simple things, such as grocery shopping, cooking, running errands, driving people to appointments, or offering child care. If your offer is not needed now, simply let them know that they can call when or if they need something. A good guideline for all of us is simply to offer, and then allow the grieving person to choose what help is needed.

4. Many, many people simply find your presence a comfort. If you are both comfortable with touch, offer a hug or hold the person's hand.

5. If you have gone through the suffering of losing a loved one in a similar way, your friend or family member is likely to know that. When he wants to talk, be ready to listen to him. It may help him tremendously to know that someone who has experienced a similar loss—for example, the loss of a child, a spouse, or a parent—has gone through the grieving process. Reassurances such as nods and simple words will often mean as much as long conversations, especially during the early phases of grief.

6. If you were close to the person who died, consider writing a note with some example(s) of what the person's life meant

to you. Many people who are grieving find comfort in notes they can read at their own timing.

7. Be sincere in your expression of what the person meant to you. While you may want to support a family member or friend, don't pretend someone meant more or less to you than she did. For example, if you were close enough to have photos of the deceased displayed at your home or on your desk at work, do not remove them solely to try to lessen someone's pain. Rarely does that help; in fact it can actually slow the grieving process to pretend the person never lived. On the other hand, if you were not that close to the person who died, do not, as a grieving person said, "suddenly build a shrine to that person."

8. As people talk through their grief with you, do not avoid mentioning the name of the person who has died. Often mentioning someone's name has a healing effect that helps the grieving process.

9. Be sparing in offering advice. What worked for you in a grieving situation may not help the other person. If you are asked for advice, you may find it helpful to preface your remarks with something like, "When I felt that way in the middle of the night, it helped me to. . . ."

10. If you share the same faith, praying together is of great help to some grieving persons. Others will not find prayer a comfort since they will be asking difficult questions about the role of God in their lives now and in the loss of a loved one. Respect a person's faith journey throughout the grief process. And, you, of course, can pray on your own or with others for strength and hope.

11. Be ready to learn from the person who is grieving. People

who are suffering and in pain are too often dismissed as having no contributions to make. Do not expect them to make a predetermined contribution to your life, but be open and ready to receive any information they may freely offer. Perhaps it will be an insight you will later value.

While listening to the grieving person, you may discover information you never wanted to know about the deceased. For example, someone you held on a pedestal may suddenly be presented a few steps lower than you had thought. On the other hand, you may learn of a touching deed the deceased performed. Either of these insights can be helpful as we remember to love people as whole people—with strengths and weaknesses.

12. Be genuine. Don't let these guidelines become rules for how you will respond. Offer what you have to offer—simply, sincerely, patiently.

A Few Words About Children and Death

If a child has lost a friend, a sibling, a parent, a grandparent, a teacher, a classmate, or other significant person, you may need to learn their "language." Many children are by nature curious and very honest, and you may be disarmed by some of their questions. Some children will ask, "What is dead like?" At a funeral, some will ask questions such as, "What is in there?" referring to the hearse. They are not being impolite; they are being themselves.

Some of the toughest questions children can ask are about God and about what has happened to the person who has died. Be honest and clear in your answers. One of the best ways to answer a question like, "Where is Grandma now?" is to ask the child, "What do you think?" Some children just need reassurance that what they are thinking is natural.

Depending on the child, she or he may be frightened or confused about death. If you are in a position to have further conversations with the child, you may want to answer, "I think Grandma is in heaven, and we can talk more about that."

Many children are shielded from death, and a caring parent or guardian will know how much a child can comprehend. Be supportive of the child's comprehension and sensitivity level. Know that funeral directors are used to inquisitive children. Many, many books are available through your local library that explain death to children. Reading age-appropriate books with them can assist them in dealing with death.

Euphemisms often confuse children, because they operate on such a literal level. If you say, "Your mom is sleeping," or "We lost Eddie this morning," they will wonder when Mom is going to wake up again or they may go out looking for Eddie, thinking he needs to be found. When I was a child, I attended my grandfather's funeral, where many of the older men talked about how my grandfather had "bought the farm." After the funeral, I assumed it was now time to go see my grandfather's new purchase. Not only was I confused, I was sorely disappointed Granddad hadn't really bought a farm.

Generally, if children are treated with respect, given honest answers, and encouraged to feel *their* feelings and express them, they can face death as well as adults do.

Introduction to the Grief Stories

I wish I could
borrow your ears
to hear the voices
I hear through
these stories.
To hear the sadness,
the gladness,
the hope,
the fear,
the trepidation,
the pauses,
the courage
of all who have
heard death.

With Those Who Grieve

∽

I long to take
your eyes
to offices,
living rooms,
kitchen tables,
bedsides,
front porches,
grimy neighborhoods,
manicured lawns,
to see the tears,
the smiles,
the glows,
the wondering,
the certainty,
the trust
of all who have
seen death.

I wish
I could take
your hands
to feel the
clammy handshakes,
the warm embraces,
the outstretched hands,
the cold,
the too-hot,
the emptiness,
the fullness,
the paradoxes

Introduction to the Grief Stories
∞

of all who have
touched death.

I wish I could
borrow your mouth
to taste
the barrenness,
the cotton mouth,
the quietude,
the emptiness,
the peace,
the beliefs,
the doubts
of all who have
tasted death.

I long
to transport you
to places
that smell
of fresh-baked bread,
of emergency rooms,
of formaldehyde
mixed with sweet flowers,
of trust,
of despair,
of urgency,
of denial
of all who have
smelled death.

With Those Who Grieve

But I cannot.
So I must count
upon these stories
and your heart
to hear,
to see,
to feel,
to taste,
and to smell death.
And hope that you
will find some
piece of that which
you seek to know.
To find a companion
for your journey.
So that through
it all we can
help each other
step out into
the glorious
beckoning
of Life and
Light.

Blessings,
pilgrim,
on your journey.

—Kay Soder-Alderfer

Sometimes Life Just Hurts
Christopher

This interview is with nine-year-old Christopher, whose best friend, Danny, died just over a year ago.

My best friend now is James. Last year my best friend was Danny. I don't think I'll ever have another friend like Danny. We used to walk to school together, and play together after school every day, and catch bugs together in the summer and put them in jars. Then we let them go, because Danny said living things didn't belong in jars.

We both liked baseball, and played on the same team. I was a pitcher and he was a catcher. We'd play catch whenever we could. We'd tell each other jokes and stories. But we didn't laugh at each other.

Danny got a bad cold. He went to the hospital where the

doctors and nurses tried to help him get well. Then one day he got cancer. He said it was like bad pinches inside. He cried a lot. I didn't laugh because I knew he really hurt bad. Sometimes I cried, too. My mom got nervous, but I told her I just felt sad.

He had to get lots of X-rays and take medicine that made his hair fall out. Sometimes he would get better and come to school. Some bigger kids laughed at him because he was bald like my Uncle Frank. They called him names like "Gramps." Danny wore a baseball cap, but you could tell he didn't have much hair.

I talked to my mom and dad about getting my head shaved so Danny wouldn't feel so funny. My mom didn't like the idea. Maybe she thought I would get cancer. I don't know. My dad took me to the barber's shop with him. I got all my hair shaved off. It felt weird at first. But I got used to it.

I went to Danny's house with my White Sox cap on. I rang the doorbell and surprised Danny. He started laughing and laughing. It was worth it just to hear him laugh. Some people thought I was making fun of him, but Danny knew I wasn't. We went to school together, and then the older kids called us "Grandma and Grandpa." Danny told me to walk like an old man, and we carried sticks. We pretended they were our canes. But later it didn't feel very funny.

Mostly I remember some special days with Danny. I remember winning a game by pitching a shut-out. He ran from behind home plate and handed me the ball. The umpire said we had to return the ball, but Danny talked him into letting me keep it.

Another one I remember was the day he told me he was dying. I told him he wouldn't, but he said his doctor told him he was dying. I got mad at him and called him a "liar." Then I ran home and cried. I was on my bed crying, and the door opened. It was Danny and his mom. I yelled, "Get out, get out!"

Danny just stood there. "I hate you," I yelled at him. I hurt inside now when I think I yelled that. Danny didn't leave my room. He looked at his mom and I guess she just knew we had to be alone.

I kept yelling, "I hate you, I hate you, I hate you for dying." All Danny said was "I know." And he picked up my baseball mitt, and came over by my bed. We were just quiet for a while. "I don't want to die," Danny said, "Honest." I felt crummy. Finally I said, "I don't hate you."

Danny said, "I know. Sometimes life just hurts." He was always saying stuff like that. I mean, stuff like adults might say. At the time it doesn't make a lot of sense, but later when you remember it, you know it's something important.

I remember going with Danny to see a Cubs game. Danny liked the Cubs, and I liked the White Sox. We were always collecting and trading baseball cards. He'd give me his White Sox cards, and I'd give him my Cubs cards. We went to Wrigley Field. Before the game we went to see some of the players near the dugout. Danny asked some of the players to sign his baseball cards, and they did. Then a couple players signed a ball, too. I think that was the happiest I ever saw Danny.

After the game we went home, and Danny was real tired. I sat next to him while he took a nap. I thought about all the good times we had. And 'specially that day. When he got up, Danny looked sick. He said to me, "I want you to have this," and he handed me the baseball he had. I said, "No, it's your baseball." Then he said I was the best friend ever, and he wanted me to remember him with that baseball. Finally I took it. I tried to think of something he'd want of mine, but I couldn't think of anything.

Another day is kind of hard to talk about. It was Danny's eighth birthday. A few guys and Danny and me were at his party. When they brought the cake and we were singing, "Happy Birthday," I looked at Danny. I could tell he hurt a lot and was tired. He looked at the candles a long time. He could barely blow out the candles. I think he knew it was his last birthday. He turned to me and asked, "Wanna know what I wished for?" I felt sort of sick. "No," I told him, because I always heard if you told anyone your wish, it wouldn't come true. He started to tell me, and I covered my ears with my hands. But I still heard him say he wished he would live until he was nine.

I just went crazy. I yelled at him, "Why did you tell me your wish, stupid? Now you'll never live another year." I was yelling and crying, and Danny's dad came and held me. I yelled some more, and I finally ran home. I cried all night long. Danny died two months later.

Sometimes I feel bad I yelled. I feel guilty a little. For a while, I used to feel like I made him die because he told me his wish. I don't feel that very often anymore, because my parents and Danny's dad have told me that he would have died no matter what. But when I had my ninth birthday this year, I got real sad again. I go to a counselor every once in a while, and it helps to talk to her.

I remember the day of Danny's funeral. I walked in and saw him in a casket. All I could think about was catching bugs together and how Danny used to let them out of jars. I wanted to help him out of his casket. I wanted him to play and laugh. But I guess I knew he was dead.

I cried a little. Sometimes I still do. Then I went up to his mom and asked her if I could leave something for Danny in the casket. She cried a lot, but said I could. I had bought Danny a Ryne Sandberg rookie card for Christmas, but he died right after Thanksgiving. I had put it in my pocket before we went to the funeral home. I don't know, I guess I thought it would keep me company. I put it in the casket next to Danny. I thought maybe Danny would know he was really my best friend if I gave him that. It made me feel good and real sad at the same time.

I don't remember too much else that day. Everybody mostly cried and whispered. My mom put her arm around my shoulder. I remember that. It felt nice. I guess that's about all you can do besides cry. Dad asked if I was OK. I cried a little, but then I nodded my head that I was all right. I remembered the time Danny said, "Sometimes life just hurts." I never told anyone, but sometimes I think dying just hurts too. It hurts everybody.

There are some wonderful "pockets of hope" in Chris's story. The adults in his life did not interfere, but rather assisted (and continue to assist) Chris in facing his grief. He still misses Danny, and is likely right that no one will mean quite what Danny meant to his life. If children are allowed to grieve freely, they heal in marvelous ways we can all learn from.

Adults—many times out of love, sometimes out of their own hurt and fears—do not allow children to grieve. Many are afraid that grieving is harmful to a child; Chris and his parents knew that exactly the opposite was true.

Beloved Mothers
Bella

Bella is fifty-four years old. As she speaks, her voice and facial expressions alternate between sunshine and storm. Her birth mother abandoned her when she was a week old. She grew up knowing her adoptive family as her family.

Her birth mother located Bella in 1969 when Bella was thirty. Her birth mother moved close by, and in 1975 Bella helped her through her dying process from an unidentified disease. Three years later, Bella's adoptive mother was diagnosed as having cancer, and Bella also helped her through her dying process. Strong emotions—from rage to tender love—erupted during both of these times.

I was born in a small North Carolina town in 1939. My birth mother was fifteen years old. A week after I was born, my mother, Shirley, left me on the steps of a hospital with a note asking them to find me a home. Then she left for the north. Now I can be calm telling that part of my life; I used to cry or get real mad talking about being abandoned.

The woman I call my mother, Ruth, worked in housekeeping at the hospital part-time. She found me and, because I'm black, took me to the only black doctor who worked at the hospital. The doctor told Ruth that she could take me home if she wanted, until they worked out some way to track down my birth mother or found a family to adopt me.

My adoptive parents, Jason and Ruth, kept me at their home while some search went on to find my birth mother. Ruth said no one much cared about another black baby. She and Jason adopted me when I was about six months old.

So, I grew up during my childhood thinking I was Bella Johnson, daughter of Jason and Ruth. I had three brothers and a sister. Jason and Ruth were both very hard-working people, taking jobs wherever they could. I loved my family very much. We lived very simply, but we always had food to eat and, usually, nice enough clothes to wear.

My dad couldn't read, but he made us all go to school, at least through eighth grade. He loved music and would carve and make us simple instruments. Probably his most valued possession was an old harmonica. My brothers and sister were older than me, and my parents were in their forties when they adopted me.

My mother would always read us the Bible at night. I remember she used to read me the story of Moses in the bulrushes often. She'd tell me how hard it must have been for Moses' mother to give him up, and the great things Moses went on and did with his life. I thought it was one of her favorite stories.

When I was thirteen, she told me how she found me like Moses was found, and how she and Jason had adopted me. She said God would help me do anything I wanted. I didn't believe her for a long time. I didn't want to. Being raised in the South, I didn't see that I could do whatever I wanted to do with my life. I was called a "nigger" and worse. I was angry that my birth mother didn't want me. I got afraid that Jason and Ruth might not want me either. But they did love me, and they will always be my father and mother.

Jason died when I was sixteen. My brothers and sister were all married and gone by then. So it was just Mama and me. My mother started to have problems with her back, so she gave up her job at the hospital. I worked some odd jobs, and finally quit school. I had wanted to be a teacher, but I gave up that dream.

When I was twenty, my mother told me I should find a husband and have a family. She and I were very close, and I didn't have any feelings for settling down. Maybe because I felt abandoned by my birth mother and some by Jason's death. I think I was afraid that if I did find someone, they'd abandon me too.

I worked in the hospital in the kitchen, and I met my husband there. We were married in 1961. I was twenty-two, and he was twenty-five. The one thing I insisted on was that if I married him, my mother was going to live with us. My mother kept her little house, and we lived with her a short while.

After my first son, Jake, was born, my mother said it was time for me to go live my life. We moved a block away. We had two more children, a boy, Moses, and a girl, Phoebe. I was determined they would never feel abandoned.

In 1966 my husband lost his job. My mother moved in with us and helped to take care of the children while I worked full-time. I remember one night walking home from work having this strong feeling of love for my mother. And the words, "She is always there" jumped into my head and made me cry and cry. If I described my mother it would be those words.

In 1969 my birth mother, Shirley, moved back to her hometown nearby. I had no idea who she was. I had taken my GED and changed to an office job at the hospital. One night when I came home my mother had dinner waiting. We ate, but I could tell she was upset.

Later when the kids were in bed, she had me sit down with her. She told me she had found out that a woman was looking for the daughter she had to give up for adoption thirty years before. I just looked at my mother and said, "Oh, no!" I didn't want to meet her even if it turned out she was my birth mother. I didn't want to feel all those old feelings of abandonment.

One Sunday afternoon, Shirley, my birth mother, showed up at our house. I had no idea how she found me, and I didn't want to know. Ruth met with her for about half an hour. I sat on the back porch.

Ruth came out and sat down next to me. She said that she was pretty sure Shirley was my birth mother. She suggested that she and my husband take the children out for the afternoon, and that I meet my "real mother." I cried, and said to Ruth, "You are my real mother. I don't need to meet that other woman." But Ruth and my husband took the kids for the afternoon.

I remember walking into the kitchen and seeing the woman who was, perhaps, my birth mother. Since I found out I was adopted, I thought my birth mother was like a huge, ugly monster. When I saw her, I was surprised at what a beautiful and delicate woman she was.

She told me how she had gotten pregnant at fourteen. Her family found her an embarrassment, and her father beat her when he found out she was pregnant. She said the easiest thing was to give birth to me at an aunt's home in a nearby town.

She wanted to run away with me, but decided she couldn't take care of me. So she left me at the hospital. She cried most of the time she talked. My heart felt divided into tiny pieces, but I was also angry. I refused to accept that she was my mother.

"So why are you here now?" I asked. "I had to see my baby,"

she said. I told her I wasn't a baby, I didn't know if we were even related, and I really didn't care if we were. I had been raised in a loving family. That was my family. I told her I never wanted to see her again. She left and I cried harder than I had in my life.

She moved into the town next to ours. I think I would have moved out of state, except my children wanted to stay with Ruth. My husband wanted to stay put, and I remember the promise I made never to abandon my children.

I didn't see Shirley for five years. Then one day my boss walked into my office and said, "Your mother is in the emergency room." I thought she meant Ruth, and I ran down to the emergency room. I heard a woman screaming in pain, and I told the staff it was my mother. I got a strange look from one of the women there who had known me and Ruth since I was a child. When I walked in, it was Shirley.

Somehow at that moment I knew Shirley really was my mother. I held her hand and whispered calming words to her. She was admitted to the hospital, but they never knew what was wrong with her. She just got worse.

News carries fast in towns like ours. Ruth heard about my birth mother and finally asked me what I was going to do. I told her I didn't plan on doing anything. Ruth was quiet a long time. Then she told me that if I had enjoyed life at all, I had to thank the woman who gave me life. I remember saying, "She may have given me birth, but you and Jason gave me life." Ruth said I had become a very bitter person. "Can't you be glad you had the love of two mothers?" I couldn't answer her. I didn't know what I felt.

A month later I met with my children, my husband, and Ruth. Ruth helped explain the situation. "I want to bring her to our house to take care of her. But I want to know what you all think." Ruth must have had them better prepared than I thought, because they all agreed it was a good idea.

My birth mother spent the last six months of her life at our home. That was a hard time for me. The doctors told me that they really didn't know the cause of her illness, and that the best thing I could do was help make her as comfortable as possible. I didn't feel like bringing her comfort. Some days I would pity my birth mother. Some days I would feel flashes of rage and scream at her. I was angry and sad and confused. I found it hard to forgive her, and she knew it.

The day before she died, she cried and begged my forgiveness. I looked at her and didn't see a grown woman who was a monster, but a scared teenager who did the best she could for me. I crawled into the bed beside her, held her, and rocked her. For the first time in my life, I called her "Mother." I laid next to her for a couple of hours, and my bitterness started to leave. She died in her sleep.

They took her to the hospital for an autopsy. The doctors asked me a lot of questions I couldn't answer. I didn't know even the simplest answer. They asked me if she had been to the islands. They thought she might have died from a rare tropical illness. I had no idea where she had spent most of her life.

The official cause of death was listed as "unknown." Later I would think that there was something very true about that; I felt my own birth mother was unknown to me. I remember walking out of the hospital after I signed papers for the autopsy. My birth mother had left me to live a better life by leaving me on the steps of the hospital. "Now maybe she'll have a better life somewhere else," I thought as I left her body at the same hospital.

Three years later, Ruth, the woman I knew and loved as Mother, was diagnosed with cancer of the pancreas. I took her home to die. A visiting nurse helped me. Mostly Mother just slept from the pain medication she was given. I slept on the sofa next to her bed. I tried to bring her simple comfort.

Twice she asked me to read to her from the Bible. And once I read to her the story of Moses in the bulrushes. She smiled faintly. I spent a lot of those last hours remembering times with this woman I loved so much, and who loved me. She died after three and a half weeks.

When I visited the cemetery a few years back, I visited Jason's and Ruth's graves. I felt a tenderness toward these people I knew as Mother and Father. Then, I went over to the corner of the cemetery where my birth mother is buried. I looked at the headstone giving her name and her birth and death dates. I wept and wept—I guess for love unknown. And because I watched two mothers die. Then I went to the caretaker's home. I asked that a line be added to her simple headstone. It now reads: Beloved Mother.

What People Don't Know
Rosa

Rosa is seventy-eight. Four years ago her husband of fifty-five years, Jacob, died at home in the middle of the night. She tells her story simply and with tenderness, and yet with a deep and powerful conviction in her beliefs about life and death.

Jacob and I grew up together in the same small town in Iowa. We went to school together until he quit to start heading his family's farm. I didn't really know him that well since he was about five years older than I was.

When I was eighteen, I saw him at a festival our town held every fall to celebrate the harvest of the year. He was there with a friend of his, and during the picnic lunch he came over and talked to me. We had a nice time, but I wasn't thinking about marrying then. I was helping my family run their general store.

61

With Those Who Grieve
ᥫᩯ

I didn't have any idea I'd marry Jacob. I can't even remember how we started courting, but after a short while he asked me to marry him. I told him I'd think it over. He seemed to be a nice young man, so after he asked my father, I said yes.

We were married for over fifty years. What I found most surprising about that was that when we got married, I really didn't think many people lived past sixty. And now I'm almost eighty!

We lived on the farm for about ten years and had our first two daughters there. It was a nice time for all of us. His brother wanted to farm, too, and after about a year, we left the farm for a bigger town with work for Jacob. It was a small city, but a big change for us. We bought a cute little house, had two more girls, and ended up living in that same house our whole life.

Jacob did a lot of outdoor work, so he was really healthy. I don't think he even ever had the flu or a cold. When the girls were children and had the measles and chicken pox, he'd stay up with them all night. I don't know when, but sometime along the way I just stopped worrying about him. Jacob was always just fine.

February 3, 1989, he seemed to have a cold and went to bed early. At 2:30 in the morning on February 4, he got up and said he wasn't feeling too good. He went to the bathroom, and when he didn't come back to bed, I got up. He was lying on the sofa in the front room. We held hands and talked a while. He asked me to rub his forehead.

In the middle of a sentence, he stopped talking. I thought he had relaxed and fallen asleep. Then I looked and saw his eyes were open, but there wasn't any life left in them. I held his hand a while more, and it started to get cold. I said a little prayer out loud, and then took my hand and closed his eyes.

What People Don't Know – Rosa

I called the pastor of the church where we belonged for forty years, and called my doctor. The doctor came first, took Jacob's wrist for a pulse, and then just said, "He's gone, Rosa." I later remembered how strange those words were, because while I was pretty sure Jacob was dead, I don't think I thought of him as being gone. He was still there, on the sofa.

The pastor came and said a few prayers with me. Then he called the funeral home. The doctor said Jacob died of a heart attack. The time on the death certificate read 3:41 A.M. My daughters all had children of their own, so I didn't want to call and wake them in the middle of the night. The funeral home people came about a half hour later, I think. It's hard to keep time straight when someone dies. The first time things became real for me was when Jacob was taken out of the house by the people from the funeral home.

By six in the morning, everyone had left and I knew I had to call my daughters. I called Julia, who lives only a few miles away. She came right over. She was probably the right one to call, because she likes to run things and she's good at it. She called her sisters, made me some coffee, and talked to the funeral home and the pastor. She stayed with me the whole day.

I remember how empty the bed felt that night.

In April I found the Valentine card that Jacob would have given me if he had been alive February 14. He had already signed it. I only cried a few times. I don't feel, though, that I pretended Jacob wasn't dead. Two of my daughters worried I wasn't grieving enough. Some friends kept saying, "Call me when it hits you." I remember thinking that whoever said that to me next I was going to ask, "What's IT?" No one ever said that to me again, though.

I had one widow friend invite me to a group for women who

lost their husbands. I guess it helped some people, but after a few times I knew the group wasn't right for me. I don't believe I "lost" Jacob. He's with me lots of times in my memories, and I talk to him out loud as if he's still with me. Because he is in my heart. Maybe it's because Jacob and I both believed so much that we would be together after we died.

I guess we all believe differently. Most of those women in the group either believed they'd never be with their husbands again, or they had to wait until they died to be with them. And I know some of them hoped they would never be with their husbands again. I didn't tell them how to feel, but I kept feeling people were telling me how I should feel about Jacob dying.

I know he died; I was there. I just don't feel like there's anything to be sad about when I know we had such a good life. So I just go on living every day being thankful for what I've had and still have. God hasn't changed because Jacob died. Maybe that's what people don't know I believe.

You Can't Play Catch with a Memorial Plaque

Phil

Phil is almost eleven years old. Two and a half years ago his father, Ross, died during a rescue attempt as a firefighter. While Phil is enormously proud of his father, he also talks about how very difficult it can be for a child to have a dead hero for a father.

You would really have liked my dad. He laughed a lot, told great stories, and did little things to make you know he loved you. He was proud of me as his son, and he loved his work, his friends, and my mom and me. He was fun to be around. A lot of my friends used to hang around him, and he would tell us stories about firefighting.

One of the days I felt happiest and proudest was when my

dad gave my school class a tour of the firehouse. The kids thought it was really neat that my dad was a firefighter. I remember one kid, George, came up to me that day and said, "You're lucky to have your dad. My dad just goes into this boring office and works all day."

I used to hang around the firehouse a lot. Sometimes I'd stop on my way home from school, and sometimes I spent Saturdays there. All the guys—and two women—used to treat me like I was someone who mattered. I'd listen to them laugh about "saving" Mrs. Thomas's cat every other week, as well as tell their stories about the big fires they fought. No one had ever died fighting a fire from his firehouse. I knew a couple of guys who broke their legs or arms helping to rescue people, but nobody ever died.

My mom used to worry a lot about my dad being a firefighter. Sometimes they'd argue about it, but they usually kissed and were friends again. Sometimes when the fire siren went off, my mom would say a little prayer that everyone would be safe. After they fought a fire, my dad would call and say that everyone was OK. He got teased some for that by the other guys, but I found out later that a lot of them respected my dad for doing that.

I guess the only thing I didn't much like was my dad's work schedule. He'd be home for three days, and then spend four days and nights at the firehouse. He'd have his meals there and sleep there. He'd call us almost every night to say, "Good night." Sometimes he'd get real mushy with my mom, and I'd just go in the other room and do my homework or play.

He also got furloughs now and then. That meant he got ten or twelve days off in a row. The first few days he'd always sleep a lot, but then we'd do stuff together as a family. Sometimes he'd take my mom out for dinner. He'd take me fishing or to a movie or play catch. Furloughs were real special times. It was like everything just stopped for the three of us. And then it would be back to his old routine.

I was in school the day he died. There was a bad fire at two houses. My dad heard a baby crying and went into one of the houses. His best friend, Alex, said that my dad saved the baby and went back into the house. He got hit by a beam that fell. Alex and another guy, Willie, went in and got my dad. He probably died from too much smoke. I'm glad he didn't burn up. He had gotten some other burns before, and even though he was a strong man, I'd hear him moan at night from getting burned.

Until that day I had always wanted to be a firefighter. Now I'm not sure. For a long time after that, whenever a fire siren went off, I'd just cry and cry.

At his wake, my mom told me I'd have to be real brave. My grandmother told me that I'd have to be the man in the family now. I was only eight years old! I tried, but I couldn't be my dad.

I saw a lot of the guys and both women firefighters at the wake. I don't think they knew what to say. Some told me that I must be very proud of my dad. I was proud of him, but I was proud of him and happy while he was alive. Now I was very sad. A lot of them were crying. I heard some of them sitting around talking about how it could have been them. Later I remember once wishing it *had* been one of them. Some said my dad was the kindest and bravest guy they knew. I started crying because it hadn't mattered that he was kind or brave. He was still dead.

The funeral was really something else. I had been to two funerals before, and they were nothing like this. All these firefighters were in uniform. I didn't know half of them. There were enough flowers to start a flower store. Someone said there were about 500 people at the funeral.

My mom cried a lot. I tried to think of what my dad would do, and I put my arm around her. It seemed to help her. I remember wishing I had a dad like George's who just had a boring office job.

A lot of what really happened is fuzzy. I was glad to see my teacher and some kids from my class. About four people talked about my dad. I do remember that when Alex was talking, he started crying. I felt then I could just be me—not a fake brave kid. I missed my dad, and I was glad that I could cry.

This may seem strange, but one thing that bothered me was, after the funeral, they put all the flowers all over a fire engine. Then they put my dad's casket on top of the fire engine, and drove all the way to the cemetery that way. I was glad when we got to the cemetery, because I was afraid his casket would fall off the top of the fire engine.

About a month later, Alex came by and drove my mom and me to a special ceremony. There were maybe only fifty people there, and I thought, "They sure forgot my dad in a hurry." A picture of my dad in his uniform was given to the fire chief. It hangs up at the firehouse. At first I couldn't stand stopping in there and seeing my dad on the wall. Every once in a while I'll stop by now, and I like seeing his picture there.

They gave me and my mom a memorial plaque for his bravery. I used to have it in my room, but one day a friend came over to play and said, "Wow, that's really neat." I got real mad. I guess I had tried to be too brave. I took the plaque down and threw it at the floor. I yelled, "You can't play catch with a memorial plaque!" And I started crying and crying.

My mom called Alex. Alex held me while I screamed and

yelled and cried about how much I missed my dad. He just held me and nodded. When I was done, Alex said, "I miss him, too, Phil. I really do." For about a minute he and I cried together. I felt a lot better.

The plaque is in the living room now. About a year ago, Alex brought me my dad's hat and jacket. That night I wore them to bed. I have his hat out on a shelf now, and his coat is in a box in my closet. Each day gets a little better. Lots of times I don't think about him dying. But then a fire siren will go off, and I say a short prayer that nobody will die in a fire that day. Especially no one's dad.

My Grandmother's Name Is Dorothy

Gail

Gail is in her early thirties. Her story was told to me in several pieces throughout the last few weeks of her grandmother's life, as well as the weeks and months following her death.

How are you?" has got to be one of the most stupid questions people can ask when they know you are losing someone you love or grieving their death. Still, people ask it. Maybe they don't know what else to say. But when people asked me that, knowing that my grandmother, Dorothy, was dying, I wanted to say, "My grandmother is special to me. She's dying. How do you think I feel?" I'd just say, "OK," or, "Not too good today." Usually they had walked away by then anyway.

Many people would say to me, "I'm praying for you," or "I'm praying for your grandmother." Many of them were sincere. But I started to feel like my grandmother was losing her own identity before she had died. It was like instead of being Dorothy, a person in her own right with her own identity, she was an appendage to me. I'd ask people to pray for her by name: "Please pray for her as Dorothy." I think some people understood that was important to me.

My grandmother had been ill, then rallied, then was hospitalized again. I knew her as a warm, vibrant, and feisty woman. And I loved her dearly. But after her second hospitalization, we found out that she had a terminal illness. My mother and dad decided to bring her to their home to live out the rest of her life. Arrangements were made for hospice care workers. The dining room was cleared of furniture, a hospital bed was put in the dining room, and my grandmother was brought home to die. The doctor estimated she had two to three weeks to live. She died two and a half weeks later.

The hospice workers helped in a lot of ways. I wish, though, that they hadn't told us one thing: They said there was a real possibility that Dorothy would rally one last time and seem like the Dorothy we knew. I held on to that hope daily. But it turned out to be a false hope I would have rather not had. Day after day I expected to see that feisty woman I so loved. I never did.

After my grandmother died, my mother wrote down some of the things she knew were important to my grandmother, for use at her furneral. Then she went over what she had written with the immediate family. We all agreed that her friends meant much to her, that she treasured her family, and that one of the things that made her uniquely her was how she had memorized the Bible verses used at the confirmation of people she cared about. We also knew she would have wanted her grandchildren and friends mentioned at the service. We all expected the presiding minister to honor her as Dorothy by mentioning these things at her funeral.

About thirty minutes before the service, the pastor told my mother that the list she had made was not appropriate at a funeral, that those things would be better put in a death notice in the newspaper. My mother, grieving at the time, was too shocked to say anything.

What shocked, angered, and hurt me the most was that throughout the funeral, the pastor never once said my grandmother's name. The funeral could have been for anyone. He kept referring to my grandmother as "the loved one," "the deceased," and "the dearly departed one." It was so impersonal. I wanted to stand up and scream, "My grandmother's name is Dorothy!"

He did mention my grandmother's love of confirmation verses, but that was only because it was something religious. Even then, he never mentioned her by name. He said, "Her daughter told me that . . ." There was so much more to my grandmother. He wasn't rude or mean. There wasn't anything *wrong*; there just was a lot that wasn't right. It was a generic, one-size-fits-all funeral. And it didn't fit my grandmother.

You can do strange things when you grieve. I remember being at the cemetery and seeing the grounds crew hanging around trying to hide by a nearby tree. When the graveside service was over, I went back to my car but waited to leave. I knew that when I left they would lower her body into the ground. Somehow I thought if I just stayed there forever I could stop the men from putting her into the earth. It seems foolish now.

After a few days away from work, I was ambivalent about going back. On one hand, I didn't want to hear a lot of people give me their condolences. On the other, I knew that I needed to hear some comforting words from people who knew what I had been through. The hardest thing for me was hearing things like, "Well, isn't it wonderful that she lived such a long life?" or "Remember, she didn't suffer long." The hardest remarks for me were either said or implied messages that I was too old to be that upset over my grandmother; it would be different if it had been a parent or my sister. Why? Why, if you love someone, does age matter at all? Who can say how much you should hurt when someone you love dies?

Three months later . . .

Some things have helped me get through. I now have two of my grandmother's rocking chairs. They comfort me to sit in them. Having something that belonged to her brings me some peace. I have moved from anger to sadness. I'm starting to sleep again.

My grandmother had seventeen Hummel figurines that she collected for my sister and me. My mother wrapped them all in tissue paper and numbered them one to seventeen. So there would be no favorites, my mom wrote numbers on seventeen pieces of paper. My sister and I each chose eight numbers and unwrapped the matching numbered Hummels. My mom took the one left over. It turned out to be one that my grandmother had bought when Mom was with her. For me, that was a special moment of remembering my grandmother.

The hospice care givers have been great. They've called my

mom a few times since the funeral to see how she's doing. They've made support-group information available to her. Right now Mom isn't interested, but she thinks that she might attend one in six months or a year. She knows there are people there for her.

The headstone is now in place on my grandmother's grave. That makes her death real. It makes it more final to read her name, and her birth and death dates.

I still have some sad times, but I'm starting to heal. I'm sure glad Dorothy was my grandmother.

At Least I'm Alive

Jean

Jean is forty-nine. Eight years ago, her older sister, Cory, committed suicide. She told her story of grief dispassionately, almost automatically, in a monotone.

It must be nice to feel like you're someone special. I wouldn't know much about that. Cory was always the one that my parents doted on. I spent most of my life trying to catch up with her, trying to prove I was as good as Cory. I became a doctor, but even that paled in Cory's shadow.

Eight years ago, she put a shotgun in her mouth, pulled the trigger and finally ended her tortured life. By age forty-five, she had had four husbands and four divorces. She was living with her fiancé, Len, when she killed herself. Actually, Len was really good to Cory. Before she killed herself, Len had probably gone through at least a dozen suicide attempts by Cory. When the police filed the report on her death, even though she pulled the trigger, they said her death was accidental. I can remember saying to one officer, "If that was accidental, I wouldn't want to see an intentional suicide."

While I was growing up, I can remember my mother once saying, "Cory can do anything she wants. She's like an angel that has been blessed with talent beyond this world."

My dad was a musician, and he was delighted when Cory became a well-known concert pianist. To this day, my dad has posters and ribbons and photos of Cory on tour all over his apartment. I don't visit him very often; it's like he's stuck in a time when Cory was at her best.

What I saw for many years was that Cory did, in fact, have lots of talent. She also was dreadfully unhappy. It was as if she lived in two worlds—one minute completely content, the next minute brooding and morose. While we were growing up, there were times I felt close to her. But most of the time I think I was scared of her moods.

Cory was five years older than me. I was not a "planned child," and that was obvious to me early in my childhood. Still, for some reason, everyone counted on me to take care of the family. Everyone told me their problems, and I just listened. I had listened to Cory's problems since she was ten.

When I was eleven, and Cory was sixteen, my parents got divorced. Cory went to live with my dad in Texas. Mom and I stayed in Indiana. Lots of people felt sorry for me, but inside I was relieved. I didn't have to listen to my parents fight. I didn't have to listen to Cory's problems. I didn't have to try to keep up with Cory's moods. I didn't have to be a mediator anymore.

At Least I'm Alive – Jean

So many people felt badly that I came from "a broken home." I listened to them, but inside I knew the relief I felt. If I have one thing to thank my parents for, it was their divorce. Maybe our home was broken, but our family had been broken long before that. The next seven years with my mom, I probably felt more whole than I ever have.

I was good at school, and had lots of practice taking care of people. So, I guess med school was a logical choice. I was one of three women in my medical school class. It was tough work, but I held my own.

There was one day I will never forget. I was in the library, researching a paper for my neurology training, when I opened a journal and started reading a case study about people who were manic-depressive. I was reading about my sister! I made copies of the article and sent them to my parents and to Cory.

My mom called me and said that just because I was jealous of Cory was no reason to suggest such things. My dad wrote and said I didn't understand Cory's unusual talent. I remember laughing when I read the word "unusual." Ironically, Cory was the only one who appreciated the article. She called and asked for more information. For the first time in my life, I felt I understood Cory. I also had hope that a psychiatrist she was seeing could help.

I sent her every bit of information I could get my hands on. I'd explain medical terms. We developed a bond between us that we had never had before. I started therapy myself.

The day I graduated from med school, only Mom and Cory came. The next day I heard Cory in a recital in New York City. Her music was flawless. My dad showed up there. I remember feeling like when we were kids—that my hard work and graduation meant nothing to my dad. Cory was his greatest accomplishment. I felt like I was just Jean, someone who didn't matter to him.

Within a week, our broken family almost rallied. Cory ended up in a psych ward after trying to overdose on sleeping pills. Once again, Cory was the center of attention for all of us. The psychiatrist at the hospital had us come together for a family session. After testing and observing Cory for a week, the diagnosis was manic-depressive. I felt justified. My mother felt guilty. My father thought the doctor was wrong.

The next several years brought a lot of hurt, confusion, and feelings of helplessness. Cory started calling me when she felt depressed. She'd call at any hour of the day or night. She went through therapists faster than she went through husbands.

Cory attempted suicide twenty-two times before she succeeded. She threatened it all the time. I guess she just couldn't find peace within herself and with the world.

I remember the day I found out about her death. My dad called me at 3 A.M. He barely got out the words: "I just got a call. Cory killed herself." I remember thinking, "Oh, sure, here we go again." Because I had gotten so many false alarms, I said to my dad, "Who told you? Cory?" I could tell from his silence that he wasn't kidding, but I honestly couldn't feel any sadness or remorse. If anything, I felt a sense of release and relief.

We had a family service. My mom felt guilty—she still does. She tortures herself with questions: what could she have done, why hadn't she taken Cory seriously, was the divorce the cause of the suicide?

My dad felt his contribution to the world was Cory, and he stopped composing music for a long time. He remarried a very young woman. She looks a lot like Cory. I don't really know if he's happy.

My mother became very ill, and I took a leave of absence from the hospital to care for her. I stayed with her a year, finally leaving my job and medicine. We fought a lot. One day she yelled at me, "You think you're so special!" I yelled back, "I may not be special, but at least I'm alive."

I joined a suicide support group. It helped some. Mental illness is hard for so many people to accept. People, including my parents, are so ashamed of mental illness and of suicide. Cory's life was so pain-filled that suicide was inevitable.

I had to quit taking care of my family and everyone else for a while. That meant leaving medicine. Instead, I learned to drive trucks, and I hauled all sorts of cargo across the country. I often took backroads when I could. The open air and scenery was a healthy change from hospitals and sickrooms. I started to see life as *alive* again.

Five years later, I worked as a dispatcher. I still do. No one knows I was a doctor. No one expects me just to help them in the same ways. I'm not sure how to offer help these days. It's a lot for me to help myself.

Shortly before her suicide, my sister had a recording made of one of her concerts. I hadn't listened to it in years. Recently, a friend was visiting me and ran across Cory's record. He put it on and said, "This is beautiful. Really beautiful." I can hear her pain even in her music. I hope some day I can hear the beauty. I believe I'm getting there.

With Those Who Grieve

When I first heard Jean's story, it was nearly overwhelming. I wondered if she would ever be less cynical about life. But I now see hope in her story.

It took enormous courage for her to name her sister's illness, to reach out and find a connection they had never had. Despite denial and guilt on the part of her parents, Jean kept trying to find health for Cory and for herself. She knows that to complete her grief she had to give up a promising career in medicine, and learn to care for herself as well as reaching out for help.

Jean has heard Cory's pain; I hope, with her, that someday she will also be able to hear the beauty of Cory's life and music.

I Still Have
One Death Stuck

Charles

Charles is a vivacious twenty-two year old who is rarely upset by much of anything in his life. "My feeling is, 'Hey, by morning it will probably all change.' My wife doesn't always like my casualness, but I just can't see getting worked up over much of anything."

After several conversations with Charles, however, he spoke of a death in the past that still haunts him. He knows he's stuck in his grieving process, but says just talking helps him move a little further along.

I've been to a lot of funerals, considering I'm so young. Most of them were of grandparents and aunts and uncles. I felt close to them, but I think I got over their deaths easy. Life just went on.

With Those Who Grieve
∞

But I still have one death stuck in my heart and my brain. Every once in a while, I'll just think of Shirley and get real sad. I guess in some ways her death hit me the most.

I was in junior high. You know how everyone thinks they're ugly or funny looking in junior high. But, if I showed you pictures of me back then and you were honest, you'd say I was truly a sight. My hair stuck out about two feet from my face. I had this little face in the middle of all this hair. Everyday I woke up and wondered if I'd ever get my hair down to normal size. My mom thought it was cute. I sure didn't.

On top of looking funny, I was real shy and had almost no friends. I was scrawny and had to wear thick glasses. Lots of days I didn't even want to go to school, because I thought everybody was looking at me and laughing at me.

Then I met Shirley. I don't think there are too many people like Shirley around. I mean, your family and teachers may say things like, "True beauty or worth is inside you," but that isn't much help to a junior-high boy who feels odd. Shirley never said anything like that to me. She just helped me feel good about myself.

I think what was so special about Shirley was that she was pretty and smart and kind and popular. Still, she made time for me. She was the only other student who really talked to me in seventh grade. She always said, "Hey!" in the halls, and would smile at me.

I worked with her on a science project in seventh grade, and she took my ideas seriously and treated me like a friend. We worked together on our project for six weeks. Those were probably the best six weeks of my growing up. We called each other every day, and she wasn't embarrassed to be seen with me.

I Still Have One Death Stuck – Charles

When I was in eighth grade, she introduced me to Rod, who is still a good friend. I think Shirley knew how to bring people together who needed friends. She was always in the school paper, or winning some award, but she was never snobbish to other people.

Since I knew her awhile, I started to tell her about how I hated my hair and my glasses. She told me about a relaxer I could buy for my hair, and after I used it and got a haircut I didn't feel like I looked like a wild man. I don't think it really mattered to Shirley how I looked, but if it bothered me that much, she told me I could do something about it. That may not seem like a big deal to you, but when you're in junior high, it's a big deal. Plus, she helped me find some self-esteem. I got less shy and made some friends.

Also, she told me about contact lenses. I saved until I was a junior in high school to get contacts. Maybe that was my way of keeping Shirley alive.

After school in early November, Shirley was walking home. She was only a few blocks from her home, when she went to cross the street and was hit by a car. She was D.O.A. at the hospital. There was a picture in the paper, I remember, of the woman who hit her. She was crying and crying.

Now as an adult, I can see how a girl in the early evening was hard to see. But I kept that picture of that woman for years. I vowed some day I'd make her hurt as much as I did. I don't know. I guess one day I just laid it all aside and started taking life real casual—or tried to.

I remember Shirley's funeral. One part of it was held in the school gym. I think almost everybody was crying, the teachers and the kids. Somehow, it was supposed to help us to see her dead. I don't know if that helped me or not. Mostly I remember about a million flowers surrounding her casket. I still can't stand the smell of flowers that are too sweet to this day. All I think of is that funeral when I smell them.

Recently I had dinner with Rod. We were talking about jobs and our families and old times. Then he mentioned Shirley. I just started crying in the middle of dinner. I realized Rod and I wouldn't have been friends without Shirley. Then we talked about how much Shirley had meant to us, and we talked a little about how we wished some adults would have helped us. Now sometimes I hear about a kid being killed or dying, and the school brings in a bunch of counselors to help the kids deal with their feelings. There wasn't any adult to help me. Now I'm an adult, and I need to find help somewhere.

Just Tell Me the Truth

Ben

Ben attended a workshop I presented in North Carolina on "Teenagers and Grief." Throughout the presentation, his attention was keenly focused. After the workshop, some people gathered for individual questions. I was surprised at the interest in grief shown by so many young people.

Ben waited until everyone else had left. He asked politely if I had time to talk with him. I sat on the edge of the stage. We talked for half an hour. He had been to the funeral of his friend, Cliff, three weeks before. These are the highlights of his story.

What is it with adults? How come they're so afraid of telling the truth about dying?

I'm sixteen. Three weeks ago today I went to the funeral of my friend, Cliff. We grew up together, went fishing together, went to school together. When we were both twelve, we got rifles for Christmas. Most of the guys we knew were hunters by age twelve or fourteen. Our dads were hunters.

The day after Christmas, our dads took us out to do some target shooting. It wasn't really new to either of us, but our fathers wanted us to know how to use guns safely. In January, the four of us went for a weekend hunting trip. We both were kind of nervous around our dads, because they had been hunting for years. But we both shot a bird each and were pretty proud of ourselves. It was like we grew up a little bit that weekend.

Our dads kept at us all the time about how to clean our guns and safely load and unload them. I think Cliff must have polished and cleaned his gun almost every day. I knew how to hunt, but it wasn't as exciting to me as it was to Cliff. When Cliff shot his first deer, his dad had it mounted. Just between you and me, I don't think I could shoot a deer. Guns are no big deal where I come from for guys who know how to use them. So, I must have gone on about thirty or forty hunting trips with Cliff. Lots of times we shot at cans or bottles. Cliff knew how to shoot. He knew a lot better than me.

A little over three weeks ago, Cliff died of a bullet wound. I stopped by to get him for school, and his mom said he wouldn't be going to school that day. Nobody seemed real upset. I just went to school. When I got to school a bunch of guys I know asked me what happened to Cliff. I had no idea what they meant. Then they asked me if he really blew his brains out or what. Finally one guy told me he heard on the radio that Cliff had been shot. I just went numb. A part of me thought maybe they were playing a mean joke on me.

Then at the beginning of school, the principal announced

that Cliff had been shot and died. I got up, ran to the bathroom, and threw up. I just walked and walked around the bathroom shaking my head. Every once in a while I remember touching the cold tiles on the wall to make sure I was there. I remembered Cliff said something to me about fighting with his dad, but it didn't sound like a big deal. Then the principal walked in with my dad, and we went home.

My mom and dad sat in the living room with me and told me that Cliff had died of a bullet wound that morning. Then, they told me that Cliff had been cleaning his gun the night before. That made sense. They told me it happened at home. That made sense. Finally I asked, "But how did he get shot?" Nobody answered. I yelled, "How did he get shot?" My parents just kept looking at each other. I knew they weren't telling me something. I went up to my room.

In the afternoon my dad came to my room and told me that Cliff had shot himself accidentally in the bathtub while cleaning his gun. *In the bathtub?* I did something I never did before; I called my dad a liar. There was no way Cliff shot himself in the bathtub cleaning his gun. My dad got really mad. He told me there would be no more hunting for me for a while. I thought that was a really strange thing to say.

So, I went to the funeral parlor and there was a closed casket. All that kept going through my head was that line about, "Humpty Dumpty . . ." His parents weren't there yet. Some of my friends were outside smoking so I went out to talk to them. I found out that Cliff had left a suicide note, taken a kitchen chair, put it in the bathtub, and shot himself.

Now I was mad. Why didn't anyone just tell me the truth? You know, I was his best friend, and I had to find out from a bunch of guys outside the funeral parlor. If suicide was something new, I could understand. But Cliff was the third guy I knew to commit suicide. And I think partly it's because no one will talk about it. Not the papers. Not the teachers. Not the parents. Not even the preachers.

The next day at the funeral the preacher just talked about how great it was to have known Cliff and how happy God must be to have him in heaven. You would have thought Cliff was eighty-three years old and died of old age or something. His parents were really tore up bad, but most everyone else just sat with their hands or arms folded.

That weekend our youth group at church was supposed to meet. The preacher talked about Cliff and how we all needed to be respectful of his parents during this difficult time. I stood up and said, "Cliff was my best friend. No way did he accidentally shoot himself in the bathtub." Some kids cheered at what I said; some laughed. They thought I was trying to make a fool of the preacher. I think he already did that on his own. I just left and cried all the way home. The next week my parents worried that I'd kill myself. I didn't want to kill myself. I just wanted someone to tell the truth about my friend.

Don't Ask Me to the Party
Betty Lynn

Betty Lynn is thirty-three. Her cousin, Starr, was killed in an automobile accident more than five years ago. Her grieving continues. And Starr's death had an impact on her life that might be with her always.

Everyone loved Starr. When she and Billy Joe got married, I think my whole clan was waiting to see if she had married someone "good enough" for her. Starr was more than good enough. She seemed to love every minute of life. And everyone she met seemed a little happier for just knowing her.

She taught school, and the kids loved her. She and Billy Joe couldn't have kids, so every Christmas they played Mr. and Mrs. Santa to all kinds of needy kids. She always saw the bright side to everything. We were more than cousins; we were the closest of friends.

So, when it was going to be Billy Joe's thirtieth birthday, she came and asked me if we could have a surprise birthday party for him at our house. We spent weeks planning the party. Since all of us were about the same age, it was a big deal that Billy Joe was the first to turn thirty. We sent out invitations to the whole clan.

We decided to have an "over the hill" party for Billy Joe. Everybody was asked to wear black clothes and bring funny gifts. We cleaned the house. We checked the guest list. And, on Saturday, the day of the party, we went shopping for food and decorations. We had a cake made up like a tombstone for Billy Joe. It had black frosting, green coconut to look like grass, and read, "Rest In Peace" on top. We had black balloons and black streamers everywhere. We laughed together at how great it looked.

We had everyone park on the next block over so that Billy Joe would think he was just coming to have a small birthday dinner with a few of us. Starr was so happy that we were able to surprise him. We all had a great time teasing Billy Joe. He had a great time having such a big party and opening all of his gifts.

At about 2:00 A.M., Billy Joe and Starr started to talk about leaving. Billy Joe wanted to stay the night, which they often did. But Starr was worried about getting home to take care of their dog. They decided to drive home, and made plans for the next day with me and my husband, Jerry. They would come back on Sunday afternoon, and Billy Joe and Jerry would pack up some of the presents he was leaving and watch sports while Starr and I cleaned the house.

They had to drive about an hour to their home. Some of us that were left kept telling stories about growing up with Billy Joe. When everyone left at about three or four in the morning, I went to bed content that Starr and I had pulled off a good party.

On Sunday, we were worried that Starr and Billy Joe hadn't showed up. But we kept telling each other that they were always late. About 4:00 P.M. Sunday afternoon, the phone rang. It was my mother calling. She told me to sit down, and I did. I thought something had happened to my daddy, my brother, or my sister.

"Starr's dead," she said in a near whisper. I heard her, but asked her to repeat herself. She told me some of the story; I think I was in too much shock to hear everything. I do remember she said the roads were icy. Billy Joe was driving, and a drunk driver swerved into their lane. Billy Joe tried to get out of the way of the other car. He hit an ice patch, and his car swerved out of control. A utility pole stopped his car, hitting it square on the passenger side and killing Starr.

I didn't cry at first. I looked around the house and saw all the black streamers and balloons. The night before they had been funny; now I tore them all down and stuffed them into a garbage bag. I saw the cake that we had gotten out of the icebox. It was only half eaten, and the "Rest In Peace" was still there. I went crazy. I threw the cake out—every crumb of it. I threw out some of the birthday presents that Billy Joe had unwrapped and said he'd be back for. I threw out anything that reminded me of the party.

I couldn't get rid of enough reminders of the party. I started to vacuum and Jerry came out of the den. He looked at me like, "What are you doing?" I turned off the vacuum, and all I said was, "Starr is dead." Then I cried and cried. I think just saying the words started to make it real for me. It was real and wasn't real yet. Mostly I just was numb, like in a fog.

I asked my husband to take the garbage out to the curb,

even though garbage pickup wasn't for a few days. I just wanted anything that reminded me of that party to be out of our house. Jerry and I cried together as I tried to tell him the few details I knew. We held each other and just cried. Soon the phone calls started—either from people who had heard the awful news or people asking, "Is it true?" And by the end of the day it seemed all I had done was cry or talk on the phone. I couldn't tell the story anymore. I kept switching between believing the awful news and seeing remnants of the party that was not even twenty-four hours old.

I remember very little about the viewing and the funeral. At the viewing I do remember seeing lots of people, most of whom had been at the party. I remember seeing Starr in a casket that had to be "reversed" so you would see the left side of her face. The right side of her face had been hurt so badly even make-up couldn't cover it. The jewelry was hers, the clothes were hers, but it didn't look like her. I felt like I was in an awful dream.

The day of the funeral was the day of Billy Joe's thirtieth birthday. At the funeral, the church was packed. The last time I had been at that church was for Starr and Billy Joe's wedding. I thought about how many people Starr loved and how many people loved her. I realized how many people had been at Billy Joe's party just a few days before, and now were at Starr's funeral. I thought it was unfair that she had to die so young and so violently. I don't think there was a person there that didn't cry. At the end of the funeral, we were all ushered by the casket one last time. I still didn't feel I was saying goodbye to Starr.

It was five months later before I really realized that Starr was dead. Deedee, a woman I worked with, had a husband who had died, and I went to the wake. When I went up to the coffin, instead of seeing her husband, I imagined I saw Starr lying there dead. I started wailing and carrying on like a wild woman. Deedee's minister came over and said, "Betty Lynn, you have to learn to accept death as part of life." I was crying too hard and was too shocked by what I thought I saw that I couldn't tell the minister I was crying over Starr being killed.

A couple of years ago, Billy Joe remarried. She's nice. But I have a hard time seeing the two of them together and not thinking about Starr. Luckily, she doesn't look or act like Starr.

Recently a lot of my friends and cousins have turned thirty or forty. Whenever I'm told that a party's being planned, I ask if it's an "over the hill" party. If they say it will be, I say "Don't ask me to the party." Because all I ever think of is funerals, not parties. Depending on who the person is, sometimes I explain why I don't want to come; other times I just don't say any more than that. I doubt I'll ever want to go to another party like that. All I'd think about is Starr being killed and that awful "Rest In Peace" cake.

I've Become an Efficiency Expert in Watching People Die

Gwen

Gwen, fifty-six, a critical care and hospice nurse, stopped by my office and told me this story about a half an hour after a patient of hers had died. I have known Gwen for four years. We have worked together professionally giving workshops on dealing with grief. Usually I know Gwen as an exuberant person, with a resilient sense of humor and infectious laugh despite the potentially depressing nature of her work.

She usually carries herself tall and walks briskly. She and I have had long conversations about health care providers and the stress and burnout that can accompany working solely with critically and terminally ill people. Usually she balances this well with her grandchildren, her philosophy of the cycles of life, and a strong belief system.

With Those Who Grieve

∽

But the day of this interview, Gwen appeared at my door looking like a dried-up leaf. There was a mist in her usually clear eyes. "I want to tell you a story," she insisted, "because I need to remember, and want others to remember Bruce." This is her story.

You know, I know better. I give all the lectures and presentations about people dying all the time. They get born. They get raised. They fill in the time. And they die.

Every day people die. Who doesn't know that? But this AIDS thing is worse than anything I've seen in my nursing career. They've died in my arms crying. I've sung lullabies to some as they've died. Everybody works against time. I do, too. But I'm supposed to work against death, too, and I know I can't. Especially with AIDS.

Bruce died. A year and a half I spent with him. He called me "Nurse Ratchet" when I first knew him. Then he called me his angel of mercy. Some angel! I couldn't give him any mercy. I couldn't give him a cure. I couldn't say to this man in his twenties—in his twenties!—that his candle was going out every day. I watched him melt away, burn away in front of me. What could I do? Try to give him hope? Hope? For what? A quick death is all I wished for him, prayed for him. And still he fought.

I was trained not to get close to people as *people*. I was told it would make me a better nurse—a more efficient nurse—to see them as *patients*. So I could do what? Watch more people die faster. Day in. Day out. Night in. Night out. Do you know what I've become? An efficiency expert in watching people die. Somehow I can tell almost to the day how long terminal patients have to live when I first see them. I don't want any more death.

I live with death all the time, and yet. . . .

I've Become an Efficiency Expert in Watching People Die – Gwen

At this point Gwen suddenly became quiet. Then she cried in deep sobs. She leaned against my shoulder and I put my arm around her. I went to turn off the tape recorder with my other arm, but she shook her head.

What will I do tomorrow? Will I walk back into all of that and find another Bruce? I don't believe I could take it. I can't take it again.

You know, I knew every inch of that man's body. Strange isn't it? I knew all his scars from childhood. And the stories that went with them. I knew all his veins. I washed him when he didn't have the strength. I knew the shape of each of his toes and fingers. I knew his allergies. I knew his dreams. I knew how to calm him. I knew his beliefs. I met his childhood friends and some of his family. And I knew deep inside he was afraid he'd go to hell.

I guess what I can't stand the most is the idea that most people who will remember him will remember him with shame. Or fear. Or denial. And how long will people remember him? *For* what? *As* what? Who will they remember?

I need to remember Bruce, not just in his suffering and pain, but in what he gave to the people he loved, in what he offered the world. I knew he was in pain, but still he tried to make life hopeful. He talked to other AIDS patients and told them to keep fighting for life, whatever life they could find. He talked to his family and told them that even if they couldn't accept and love him, he loved them all. And he told everyone he met that they were worth something.

He loved music. He played the piano, he said, to soothe his soul. And when he was too weak to play, he listened for hours to all kinds of music. It got softer in the last few months. As I did. And anyone who really knew him.

With Those Who Grieve
∞

Tomorrow. Tomorrow I will rest. I don't want to go back to work again. I don't know if I want to meet another Bruce. The pain is just so, so deep. And there's nothing I can do to stop it.

Gwen took a six-month leave of absence from her work. Today she helps families with AIDS through case management, including advocating for treatment funding.

The Father I Never Had

Bob

Bob, thirty-eight, knew a little over a year ago that his father was dying of cancer. His father died six weeks prior to the following interview. Because of his family situation, he learned of his father's death the night after he was buried.

Bob's story is both poignant and remarkable as he has tried to find closure for the life and death of his father. He wanted to tell his story because he believes many people are in similar situations.

My parents were divorced when I was seven years old. After their divorce, I went to live with my mother. As a result, I never really had the chance to know my dad. My first childhood memory is of going to court with my mother, who changed her last name and mine to her maiden name. I can remember thinking, "This is pretty cool to be able to change my name."

I was my parents' only child. My mom had two daughters by a previous marriage, but they were grown up when the divorce happened. So, I lived alone with my mom. I heard her put my father down all the time, so I wasn't real anxious to get to know him. When I did see him, he tried to make up with me by giving me money instead of affection.

I was abused by my mother. Since she also worked very hard as a single parent and provided me with a home, I never questioned the abuse. If you don't know anything else, I guess you accept that as normal. Plus, I guess I'm just a survivor; I survived that, Vietnam, a divorce from my first wife, and just about every other painful situation.

A year ago Christmas, I found out that my father had cancer. To deal with that and a lot of stress in my life, I started seeing a counselor. As we talked about my family, I didn't really have anything bad or good to say about my dad. He was just someone who never really claimed me. And I never claimed him either.

As adults, we'd see each other from time to time, but we never spent any time together that mattered a lot. One of the reasons we didn't was because my stepmother is a very selfish and jealous person. She seemed to get in the way of us ever getting to know each other. So mostly my dad and I just observed my birthday and Christmas together. He always wrote a check as a gift. But I didn't want his money; I wanted to know him better.

After I was in counseling for a few months, I knew I had to say some kind of goodbye to my dad.

I drive routes for a vending company, and one day when I was out in my truck driving, I decided to give him a call. This took a lot of courage for me, but in the middle of the conversation, I said, "I love you, Dad."

That was the first time in my life that I can remember telling him that I loved him. He was quiet; it sounded like he was crying a little. I told him that I hadn't been in touch because his wife and their daughter always seemed to interfere or not pass my messages to him. He agreed to call sometime.

In a way, that was my closure with him. I had said what was on my mind. I was able to tell him that I loved him, and I claimed him as my dad.

I was pretty sure I wouldn't hear from him again. I told my counselor and a few other people close to me that I wouldn't be surprised that if he died I wouldn't know, because my stepmother would never tell me. I think everyone thought I'd certainly be told, but I never believed I would.

Six weeks ago my dad died. He died nearly a year since the last time I talked with him, the time I told him I loved him. He died on a Tuesday. The wake was on Thursday. The funeral and burial were on Friday. I didn't find out he had died until after the burial. My mother-in-law had read the obituary on Friday afternoon and called my wife that night. My wife was the one to tell me he died.

I felt angry I wasn't told, but mostly I felt like this death was different than others I had known. When people I cared about had died before, I could grieve the loss of all they had been in my life. Now, my reaction was really one of great emptiness. I felt like all I could grieve was the fact that my dad and I had not played ball together, fished together, talked about anything important. I grieved for the father I could have had, but never did.

As part of my therapy, I brought the obituary to a counseling session. My counselor asked if I could read it aloud. It took a lot of deep breathing, but I did it. Even in his obituary, I was not listed as one of his surviving relatives. No mention was made of a son, of me.

When it gets to be springtime, I plan to visit his grave. I'll take along a tape recorder and say all the things I need to say. Maybe then I'll have the closure I need. Maybe then I'll really grieve for the father I never had.

Walking Grief's Road with a Friend

Lois

Four years ago, Lois, forty-seven, found out Ryan, her friend Jill's son, was dying of cancer. She walked the road of grief with Jill throughout Ryan's dying process. She has also helped support Jill in her grief since Ryan's death two years ago.

Lois herself experienced her own grief process, as did many others. For Lois it was crucial to find support for herself as well as be supportive of Jill. She discovered that while there is support available for families with dying children, there is minimal support for friends who are both supporting the family in their grieving yet feeling their own sadness and sense of loss.

With Those Who Grieve

I know a lot of people wonder if one person can really make a difference. I learned during Ryan's brief life—and through his dying process—that we all make some difference. He was like the proverbial pebble in the lake that sends ripples far beyond where it was thrown.

Here was one little child who lived only six years on this earth, and yet his life and death touched not only his family, but friends and coworkers, those who cared for him medically, and our entire community of 30,000 people. If I learned one thing from the intense and often painful experience of his dying, I learned there is honor and dignity in walking the difficult road of grief with a friend.

I will never forget the day Jill, my friend and coworker, told me that Ryan had been diagnosed with cancer. Just days before we had been celebrating his fourth birthday. Now we knew he was going to die.

I had no immediate words of comfort. I don't think there are any. I never felt so powerless. I knew there was nothing that I could do or say that would stop the inevitable. I was stunned as she told me, for I cared both for Jill and her family. The one thing I realized was that our friendship would now take a different path, one neither of us would choose.

I had four things going for me as I faced this news with Jill and Ryan. First, I believe in God. I knew that Jill was a devout Catholic and that we would be counting on God to get us through some very tough times. I'm not sure I realized just how tough, but I know I couldn't have made it through Ryan's death without believing in some loving and powerful force beyond us.

Second, I have a personality that finds it easy to listen to people, and I can just let them be where they are and who they are.

There were days throughout Ryan's battle with cancer that would bring laughter and tears, wishing it were otherwise and dealing with reality, remissions and brief rests, long periods of pain for all of us. If Jill needed someone who would listen or give her a hug, I could do that. If Jill needed me close, that was fine. If she needed space to be alone or needed to be with her family, I respected that. I learned how important it was to respect Jill, Ryan, and their family; everyone in the family—Jill and her husband, Ryan, and their other two children—reacted differently to Ryan's impending death.

Third, as a researcher, I have both an insatiable curiosity and the know-how to tap into and make use of resources. I wrote to organizations requesting their literature. I read anything I could get my hands on that talked about Ryan's illness and grief. This helped me understand some of what Ryan would be facing, and what Jill and her family would face. On at least an intellectual level it prepared me for some of what I would be going through as well.

Fourth, I am a person who can use resources to network. Ryan was treated at a hospital with an excellent social services department. They helped Ryan and his family, and they provided those of us who would be close with resources that helped us know what to do and what not to do to help. Jill gave some handouts to us at work that I found helpful.

Even so, it was hard at times to listen to Jill's sadness and despair, not only because I cared about Jill and Ryan, but also because I was going through my own grief. Sometimes I felt I was like two people. One person was Jill's friend trying to be supportive of her. And then another person was the me facing my own grief and questions about life and death.

It is almost impossible to find a support group for people who have friends who are losing their children. Often, after listening to Jill, I would go home to my apartment, and my own grief would hit. There were times I cried over my own grief.

I turned to other trusted friends who had some firsthand experience with grief. I would call and talk with them or write to them and try to let out some of my feelings. This was not always easy for me since I'm a very private person. But sometimes I think I just couldn't hold it all in anymore.

Sometimes the best way for me to deal with my grief was to help Jill by running errands she didn't have time to do. I usually waited for her to ask, as I wanted to honor her. If I sensed she was going through a very stressful time, I would ask if she could use a hand with something.

Also, part of my whole support system was my Native American heritage with our view of the sacredness of life and the view of life cycles. I would pack up my camping gear and just go away by myself for a weekend. In the quiet, observing nature, I'd find a peacefulness. Those times helped me see Ryan's life and death as having a naturalness and meaning.

If you had met Ryan when he was four, you would have met a cherub. He had curly hair, long eyelashes, and a warm, sweet smile. To watch him change physically over two years was hard. Almost to the end, though, he stayed hopeful. In fact, a few weeks before he died, Ryan and the family went to the hospital. The staff who worked with Ryan knew he was close to death.

The family met with a psychiatrist. He asked Ryan if he believed the tumor was gone and he'd be healthy and OK. Ryan smiled and said, "Yes." He then asked Ryan how he'd feel if he knew that the cancer had returned and he was going to die.

Ryan wouldn't even answer that question. Maybe he died deny-
ing his death, but I also think a part of him carried hope inside
until he died.

Jill and her family decided that Ryan would die at home. It
was difficult for everyone. Jill knew it would mean missing work,
and I tried to be supportive of her decision. Jill hired Ryan's
babysitter to help her. Her babysitter was an enormous help. She
was so touched by Ryan's life and death that she gave up her plans
to attend law school and, instead, trained in social work to help
children like Ryan face death.

Our whole town was affected by Ryan's example. Ryan's
health care required more money than Jill's family could afford,
so the entire community held benefit events to help finance his
care. Ryan battled his cancer through surgery, chemotherapy, a
bone-marrow transplant, and finally drugs that could only help
ease his pain. When he died, editorials and testimonies to Ryan's
example of living showed how much Ryan had touched all of us.
I think anyone who was touched by Ryan's life will never be the
same again.

To help us at work prepare for Ryan's death, Jill distributed
some handouts from the hospital on some guidelines for responding to the family immediately after a child's death and for continuing to support them over time. I made a photocopy of mine,
and kept one copy in my desk drawer at work and one at home.
Later I made copies for friends who supported me as well.

About six months before he died, I started to feel that any
day Ryan might die. It was really tough to live knowing that
Ryan's inevitable death waited somewhere around a corner on the
road we had been traveling. Jill insisted we all be realistic, but also
that we celebrate Ryan's life while he was alive. Despite his ill-

ness, Ryan joined Boy Scouts and participated as fully as possible in life. He attended school when he could.

Ryan died two weeks after his sixth birthday. He died with his family, in Jill's arms at home. The family all said goodbye to Ryan there.

At the wake, Ryan was in a casket with his scout uniform on. A small stuffed animal was next to him. It helped his death be more real to me to see the body. Jill and her husband had planned the funeral months in advance. At the cemetery we all put one rose on his coffin. It was very moving for me.

The two years since have been times of slow healing. I acknowledge birthdays and anniversaries of Ryan's life, which Jill finds helpful, even if sad. It has helped me to acknowledge Ryan's life as well as his death. Ryan is still very much missed when the family does activities together; Jill has gone through physical illness and nightmares. Ryan is not forgotten. We are on a new road, but not an easy one yet. We still need to stroll slowly.

A Mixture of Shame and Grief

Paul

Paul, forty-five, is a minister in a small town in Eastern Pennsylvania steeped in Pennsylvania Dutch culture. He is a committed, industrious, compassionate man with a gentle laugh, satisfied with the simple pleasures of his family and his work. Grieving through his brother's illness and death was the most difficult battle he has faced.

It was Christmas Eve Day when my brother, Tom, called from Illinois to tell me he had AIDS and was dying.

Being a minister, that evening I would be expected to lead worship services highlighting the joy of Christmas. I didn't feel much joy that Christmas. The only thing on my mind was that my brother—my only brother—was hospitalized and was dying.

111

As I told my wife, RuthAnn, I wept tears of sadness and bitterness, tears which would characterize much of the next two years.

That Christmas I also knew what members of my parish did not yet know: It would be my last Christmas in the town where both our children had been born and raised, and where I had served the first fourteen years of my ministry. Soon our family would be moving to another town; I would be serving a new parish. It felt like a season of loss, not joy.

I am the youngest of three children. Tom was six years older than me; my sister, Dot, is eight years older than me. I am a Lutheran pastor; my sister is a nurse. My father is a retired fund-raiser for the Lutheran church; my mother is a retired nurse, showing early signs of Alzheimer's disease.

Of the five of us, Tom was obviously the most brilliant, and it showed in the books he devoured, his language abilities, and the incredible ease with which he could master a new subject. From the time he was a teen, his aspirations centered on the theater. Even four years in the Army Security Agency during the Vietnam era didn't stop him from being involved in stage work wherever he was stationed.

Five days after Christmas my parents would celebrate their forty-ninth wedding anniversary. The three of us children had planned a low-key celebration at a local restaurant. Dot would be coming from New York; Tom would not be traveling. How, I thought, am I supposed to tell everyone this news?

We met for dinner. As we made our way back from the salad bar, I pulled aside my sister. In a hushed tone to cover my shame, I said, "Tom has AIDS." She immediately realized what I had faced a few days before: Tom was going to die. It didn't matter that she and I deal with dying people all the time. It didn't matter that we both knew all people are mortal with limited time on this earth. This was Tom—our brother, Tom.

I told Dot Tom's words to me on the phone, "I got it the usual way." We quickly made the decision that now was not the time nor place to tell Dad and Mom. That would be later when they—meaning *we*—were ready.

Tom's pneumonia responded to treatment, and within a few weeks he was out of the hospital. In April of 1989, when I began working at a new congregation, I wondered how members would react when they learned my brother had AIDS. I wasn't yet comfortable telling them. I had told only my family and my closest friends.

That month, Tom was going to be at a trade show near us, and called to tell us he wanted to see our new home. He also said he wanted to have a final look at the home our parents had lived in since 1965. My parents were moving to a retirement community where there would be more help for my mother's worsening Alzheimer's. We invited Tom and my parents to come for a meal.

At that point, RuthAnn and I hadn't told the kids about Tom's illness. Megan was twelve and Colin was seven. We read everything we could get our hands on. We were both worried about the visit. Would it pose a risk to us or our children? Every book, every piece of information said no, but our fear was still there, a groundless, floating anxiety.

We didn't know Tom was afraid as well, but for an entirely different reason. When we had seen him in Chicago the summer before his revelation, he and I had parted with the big bear hug that had become our way to say goodbye. Now, he confided, he was worried I would not touch him, let alone hug him.

The men in our family have always been chunky. When we

saw Tom in the summer of 1989, he had lost some weight, but still looked like one of us. That would not last long. By the following summer anyone who saw him knew he was dying. He was gaunt, and looked like some survivor from the Baatan death march. His living death affected us all profoundly.

I told my dad of Tom's illness sometime in the months after that first Christmas of knowing. Mom, with her Alzheimer's, never has been told the cause of his death. We all knew death was inevitable, but the final months in 1990 were still rough.

I talked to Tom a lot more frequently than I ever had, assuring him both of my love and God's love for him. He moved to a third floor apartment closer to work. With a gallows-like humor, he would relate how he was not always able to make it all the way upstairs before the constant diarrhea would strike, and I would say what he needed was rubber bands around his pant legs.

In October 1990, he entered the hospital for the final time. My sister went to be with Tom in what we now suspected would be his death. We told our children of his illness; they took it surprisingly well. We encouraged them to ask us any questions, but they had few.

My sister being with Tom was therapeutic for my father and me. We felt we would do as well to stay in the East, and travel to Chicago only to clean out his apartment after his death. My decision not to go to my brother's bedside is one I now question, but at the time I was not ready for it.

A year earlier, Tom had a terrible experience at one hospital that had treated him like a leper. Now he had found a loving, caring environment at the AIDS floor at Saint Joseph's Hospital. It was there he lived out his last earthly days. Dot sat by his bedside every day. She called each day to say how he was failing physically, but maintaining his sense of humor. Dot found great support from the pastoral intern and a visitor from my brother's congregation.

Saturday night, November 10, Dot called to say Tom was near death. I knew this was it, and I hoped his death would come after—not prior to—church services that next day. I knew I couldn't handle leading worship otherwise. Shortly after lunch on Sunday, November 11, 1990, Dot called to say Tom had died.

My father, a proponent of cremation, made arrangements to have Tom's remains cremated and shipped to a funeral director friend of mine in a nearby town. Dad thought we should scatter Tom's ashes, just as he wants his own scattered. I wasn't ready for that yet; my friend said he'd keep the ashes as long as we wanted.

As it turned out, it wasn't long. The end of November, my cousin Peter, who had been close to Tom, was killed in an automobile accident. His widow decided to bury him in the cemetery next to the church I serve. She asked me to conduct the funeral and burial. We asked and received her permission to bury Tom's ashes atop Peter's casket. Cousins who had been friends in life were now united in death. It brought me some peace.

Also, by now I had told the parish of my brother's death from AIDS. I felt I also needed to ask them for permission to bury his ashes in the parish's cemetery, knowing how many fears we had faced about AIDS. They were wonderfully supportive of me, my family, and of the burial.

I faced many painful days after Tom's death. I made arrangements to leave for Chicago on November 18 to go clean out Tom's apartment. I picked up my father in central Pennsylvania, and the two of us headed to Chicago to close out my brother's apartment; arrange for and attend a memorial service for Tom the day before Thanksgiving; sell his automobile; and settle his affairs. Those days would turn out to be the longest of my life. We thought the wilderness was behind us, but we discovered it lay ahead.

By Monday afternoon we reached the suburban Chicago neighborhood next to my brother's and checked into a motel. There was a message at the motel to call home immediately. Dad was told by the supervisor of the nursing unit to which Mom had been admitted a few months previously that she was bleeding internally. She had been admitted to the local hospital.

As he got off the phone, the first tears I had ever seen from my father fell to the floor. We wondered if the death of my brother would be compounded by the sudden loss of my mother. We were a thousand miles away. As it had and would again, my anger at my brother welled to the surface along with a myriad of other emotions.

My father and I had intended to finish up in Chicago in a week or ten days. Now, prayer, the comfort of each other's arms, and resolve gave us strength to do as quickly as possible all we had planned, so we could get back home to my mother. That night as we drove over to my brother's apartment and climbed those same steps he had struggled up so many times, we came face to face with the living death called AIDS.

Tom had never been a neat fanatic, but what assailed us were the last desperate days of a man dying of this twentieth-century plague. I spent the next two days cleaning and scrubbing two months' accumulation of vomit and filth and feces. Dad spent the time making phone arrangements for the memorial service, disposing of the car, gathering bills, and doing the necessary legal paperwork to transfer accounts.

A Mixture of Shame and Grief – Paul

∞

By some miracle of God and the help of some of Tom's friends, by Wednesday morning we had my van loaded; a trash bin behind his apartment building filled; his car sold; mail rerouted; a landlord pacified; bank accounts closed; and we were greeting friends and acquaintances inside Tom's church.

I've conducted hundreds of funerals as a pastor and could never quite figure out what all the crying was about. Tom was the first close relative to die since my grandparents died when I was a toddler. Now I was surrounded by my brother's friends and coworkers, by my father, and, serendipitously, by my wife's brother and his wife, both of whom had moved to Chicago just two years earlier. We began what would turn out to be anything but a routine memorial service. It would be a day of discovery about Tom, his friends, his work, and myself.

As Dad and I completed arrangements for the memorial service, we found out the service would be led by the intern who had visited my brother and comforted my sister. She encouraged us to allow for a time of personal remarks.

I loved Tom and always would. But, until that service, the shame of his actions and death outweighed any feelings of the grace of God. Yet at that service, and later during the fellowship time that followed, each of us who mourned Tom's death was able to get a larger picture of this huge man who had shriveled to skin and bones in his final days.

A choir director spoke of Tom's love of music; a friend described his philosophical comments while overlooking the ocean; a pastor talked of his deep faith; a coworker joked that brilliant innovations at work were termed a "Tom."

My father was able to speak of Tom's proficiency in Mandarin Chinese during his stint in the Army. Coworkers said it was a skill Tom never spoke of and which remained concealed until he stunned his fellow employees on a transoceanic flight. Tom spoke that language to console a sobbing woman on the flight with whom no one else could converse.

That service allowed me to shed tears of sadness, anger, and other emotions which had grown within me. I was comforted by a brother-in-law who simply allowed me to grieve and weep for both myself and my brother. It was the beginning of my healing.

The days, weeks, and months that followed helped my restorative process as I served as executor for his estate with no will. He had never been a fantastic money manager. But the final months of Tom's life must have been a living hell as the bills piled up, while the means and desire to pay them evaporated. After spending countless hours cleaning up—both literally and figuratively—after what was once my brother's life, I finally can look back upon Tom and the last few years with a smile on my face, while I simultaneously shake my head in disbelief.

As a child, I once had threatened to one day "hire a gorilla to pounce on" Tom. Many times later we laughed at that commentary on the frustration and love we both felt. Little did we realize that the gorilla would be in the form of a plague that, in a slow and agonizing way, would eat away at the life—but never the spirit—of my brother.

When I first learned Tom had AIDS, I was appalled at what it would mean for me and the shame it might bring. As I came to grips with my own feelings, I felt my emotions start to shift away from me and over to Tom and his life, his dying, his pain.

As RuthAnn and I wrote our annual Christmas letter the year Tom died, I wrote of his death and its cause. For me, I came to a closer understanding of Christmas than in all my years of ministry. In the two years since Tom made that first phone call, shame yielded to grace. My selfishness yielded to love. As I learned to accept myself, I learned to accept Tom. Tom is at peace. Finally, so am I.

I Just Wanted
Honest Compassion

Joseph

Joseph's parents were divorced when he was three. His mother returned to the job force and had to work two jobs to make enough money to live on and raise her three sons. His aunt, who died last year, and his uncle were formative in his growing up.

Joseph is forty-seven. When his aunt died, he discovered that the "compassion policy" of his company had a very narrow definition. Part of his grief recovery was channeled into forming a more equitable compassion policy.

After my parents divorced, my mom was left with very little. She had to get two jobs to support herself and the three of us boys—Stewart was seven, Ken was five, and I was three. This was in the fifties, when there weren't a lot of jobs for women. My mom didn't complain much; she just did what she knew had to be done. We moved from Nebraska to Chicago; she said there would be more jobs there. I really admire my mom for doing the very best she could with a bad situation.

My Aunt Sue and Uncle Peter lived in Chicago too. We moved in right down the block from them. I remember spending a lot of time at their house, especially until I was a teenager.

Aunt Sue was real easy to get along with. Nothing much seemed to bother her. We could run around all over making noise, and she'd laugh and laugh. When I started school, I'd go home to Aunt Sue's and do my homework while she fixed dinner. My mom would come by around dinner time, and we'd all sit down to a hot meal. Then we'd go home with my mom for the rest of the night. The term *latchkey* wasn't used then, but if it weren't for Aunt Sue and Uncle Peter, I'd have been a latchkey child.

My Uncle Peter would take us on occasional camping outings, and he taught me to fish. He and Aunt Sue came to my games and concerts. I think maybe they both really enjoyed us because they had no kids of their own.

Last year, my Aunt Sue died of cancer. I really felt the blow of her death. I mean, she had been a second mother to me my whole childhood. She had often been the first one to pat me on the back for a job well done, for trying hard at school, and for a ballgame played well. I hadn't really felt a family death hit me that hard.

I took a week off from work for the funeral and then helped my Uncle Peter get a lot of things in order. Since my Aunt Sue had been sick so long, the house needed to be cleaned up. We took all of her clothes to a local thrift shop.

When I got my next paycheck, I found I had been docked three days' pay. I asked my boss about the shortage, thinking someone had made a mistake. She pointed out that three to five days of "compassionate time" were allowed for a family member, but the person had to be from the immediate family—parents, siblings, spouse, or children. At first, I just felt sad and a little angry that my place of employment only acknowledged those people as immediate family.

About five months later, I was at my mom's for Christmas. I walked my Uncle Peter home after dinner. As I walked back to Mom's house, I was thinking of old school friends from the neighborhood. John had been raised by his grandmother. Luther's mom was sick a lot, and so he had spent a lot of time with friends, especially for meals; my Aunt Sue had fed him at least once a week. Paul was really raised by his older brother, because his mom had left and his dad drank all the time.

I thought about how many of us were raised by people who cared about us, but who might not be called "family." I mean, I don't know many Donna Reed-type families. That got me thinking about that policy at work. Almost no one from the neighborhood would have been granted any compassionate time for grieving the loss of these people who raised and loved us.

When I returned after the holidays, I started an ad hoc committee for compassionate leave. I gave my own examples of my aunt and how I got docked pay. Yet, under that same policy I could take off and get paid for five days if my dad died. My father, who had nothing to do with my growing up and who has seen me only five or six days of my life. I don't feel close to him. Why should I be docked pay for grieving the death of someone who was more like family to me than my own father? Who can tell me how I should feel about someone dying?

The "higher ups" said too many people would take advantage of a kinder policy, so we met halfway. The policy now reads that compassionate time and full pay will be given for death and grief situations, as approved by your supervisor. A lot of people have thanked me for pushing the system. I wasn't trying to push the system. I just wanted a policy that honestly reflected compassion.

I Hope Heaven's Like Tahiti
Maxine

Maxine has been employed as a critical care nurse for ten years, and as a nursing supervisor for eight years. Her most difficult nursing challenge came when she was in her late twenties and early thirties. She provided home health care for her parents, who both died of cancer.

Maxine is a consummate professional. She speaks very deliberately, with no hint of unresolved grief. She attributes this to the close time she spent with her parents as they died, time that was "sometimes agony, sometimes honor."

When I was twenty-nine, my mother was diagnosed as having bone cancer, which is a very painful disease. Since there was only my brother and me, the caretaking fell to me. I moved into my parents' home and started what would be some of the worst and best days of my life.

As a nurse, I knew what to expect. That worked in my favor sometimes; other times it worked against me. I had taken care of a lot of terminally ill patients, but it's different when it's your parents. I thought I had gotten used to seeing pain and could pretty much go on "automatic," but when my mother was in pain, I couldn't just be a professional. It hurt me to see her suffer, and I knew that she would have worse pain ahead.

The good part of it was that I got to know my parents in a very special way. When people are dying, things start to get real basic. And while you talk about deep subjects like death and dying and what might exist after this life, it's not intellectual. It's happening.

My mother was not a religious person in terms of church attendance and those sorts of things, but she did believe that God took care of the world. I think she was deeply spiritual in that she had a faith or belief that everything would be all right. We talked a lot about what an afterlife might be like. She used to say, "I hope that heaven's like Tahiti." She meant that it would be a comfortable and comforting place that was peaceful for her. We used to laugh about that, but I was glad she found a way of comforting herself.

My mother was determined to live until Easter. A lot of terminally ill people can make it through to a holiday and then die. But I started to see how weak and sick she was the week before Easter, and I doubted she would make it.

When I first quit my job to take care of my mother, my brother told me I could count on him, and two good friends who live out of state promised their support. The Tuesday before Easter, I remember taking the telephone into the bathroom and whispering so my mom wouldn't hear. I told my brother that if he wanted to see Mom alive, he'd better come then. He said he'd be there Saturday. I called my two friends, and one took off work to come be with me. The other friend said, "Maxine, you're too tired and too dramatic. I'll get there this weekend." I cried in the bathroom, and then went back to take care of my dying mother.

My mother died at 1:10 A.M. on Good Friday, three days before my thirtieth birthday. She didn't make it to Easter. Only my one friend and my dad were there with me when she died. I was furious my brother and other friend hadn't taken me seriously. Instead of making birthday plans, I helped to plan a funeral.

Only a few weeks after my mother's death, we found that my dad had a sore on his neck that turned into a malignant, cancerous growth. His death was a lot faster than Mom's. I think now that he knew he was sick earlier, but didn't want to bother me with his illness while I took care of my mother.

I can remember being on automatic pilot with my dad. I was probably numb from the death of my mother, and I just did what came naturally to me as a professional. I changed his bandages, fed him, washed him, took care of his needs. One of the difficult things was that he could hardly talk at all because his cancer had spread to his throat. I knew there were things he wanted to say—I could see it in his eyes. He would often cry. He died within six months.

There was no way I could go back to my job as a critical care nurse. I was spent. Totally spent. My brother helped some, but mainly I was the one to take care of "cleaning up" the estate. It took three years before I was ready to walk out into life again.

One thing helped me come back: I stayed at my parents' home after my father died. I had time to spend with things that held memories of them. I woke up every night at 1:10 A.M. It was like a reminder that I hadn't really had time yet to say goodbye to my mother.

One night I was so tired that I fell asleep in an easy chair in the den. Right at 1:10 A.M. I woke up with a start. I saw a shadow outside of the window, and went to see what was going on. I saw that a window was open slightly and thought I should call the police. But something drew me to the window. Even though it was winter, I felt a warm breeze blow across me as I closed the window. All of a sudden, I remembered my mom saying she hoped heaven was like Tahiti.

I can't explain it. All I know is that I slept the night through from then on, and felt my mom was in a very peaceful place.

Two Minutes

Tina

Tina is fifty-one. When I first met her, she was a tiny, very frag-
ile-looking woman. Her face was drawn, and her eyes held very
deep sorrow. When she spoke, it was often in a near whisper or
with great sadness.

We met to talk about her feelings regarding the death of one of her
younger sisters. Through the peeling back of the years, many tears were
shed, and her eyes began to brighten. After a year, she did indeed look
many years younger.

At the time, Tina was taking classes at a local college to retrain
in a career in interior design. That was fitting. She had redesigned
her own interior by dealing with a loss that had occurred nearly
forty years before.

With Those Who Grieve

∞

I come from a family with eleven children. I'm the oldest. By the time I was eleven, I was almost mother to six brothers and sisters. My mother would have a baby, take care of the baby, get pregnant and then I would look out for the kids from the minute I got home from school until I went to school the next day.

I loved going to school, because that was about the only place I could rest. It was easy for me to get good grades, because I only had to take care of myself at school, and I had learned how to do that years before. I was very shy as a child. I think I believed if I got to know someone, I'd have to take care of them, too, and I already had enough people to take care of. I had few friends.

One day I came home from school excited about winning a writing award. It was very important to me, because the story I wrote was going to be published in the local paper. Since I was so shy with people, it was easier for me to write about my feelings and thoughts. The award was also important because it was one of the few times I had really been noticed for having any talent. It wasn't that my parents didn't care; it was just that my dad had to work all the time and my mom had to spread her attention and affection very thin over all the children.

I was told to watch the kids as usual. I tried to get my mom's attention to tell her about my writing award. She just said, "That's nice, Tina." I guess I felt disappointed I had no one to celebrate with. I remember that I sat down at the kitchen table looking at my award and feeling very proud of myself.

My sister Theresa was almost two years old and got into everything. I wanted to make sure that my award was safe from her, that she didn't tear it up or color all over it. I went to my bedroom and put it in the top drawer of my dresser. All of a sudden I heard my mother screaming, "Tina! Tina! Oh, my God, no!"

∞

I tore out of my room and went to the kitchen. My mother had pulled Theresa out of a pail of hot water that my mom was going to use to mop the kitchen floor. My mom started yelling, "Call the police! Call the police! Tell them Theresa has to go to the hospital." Theresa wasn't screaming. She was just sort of whimpering. My mother wrapped her in a blanket. I called the police, and they came and took Theresa and my mother to the hospital.

The house was as quiet as I can ever remember. All the kids just quit running around and played quietly. Every once in a while, one of them would ask, "When is Mom coming home with Theresa?" I kept waiting for a call. I felt I was growing older by the minute.

That night my mom and dad walked in the house together without Theresa. She had died from burns.

I don't remember much about the funeral or the wake, except there was this tiny little coffin with the lid closed. At first no one in the house even talked about Theresa dying. We just came home from the cemetery and went to school the next day. I remember having nightmares for a long time.

We came from a small town, so the paper ran the obituary about Theresa and never ran the story I got the award for. I remember thinking I would do anything to have those two minutes back when I put my award away. I wished that Theresa *had* torn it up or colored on it. But I always kept it. I still have it today.

You know how families tell embarrassing stories about something you did as a kid to boyfriends and strangers and other people in your family? Well, the story of how I let Theresa die was the story that people always heard about me.

One day when I was fifteen, I remember my cousins coming

to visit. My cousin Mark said to me, "Well, if it ain't Tina the baby killer." All my shame and guilt turned into anger. I hit Mark so hard I broke his nose. Another trip to the hospital. Mark was kind of proud of his broken nose, but said I'd better not tell anyone that a girl broke it. I knew Mark got more than he deserved from me, but at the time it felt good just to release the energy.

I was grounded for a week and had to spend any time at home in my room. I'd just lie on my bed looking at the ceiling, relieved I didn't have to take care of anyone. It was more like a vacation than punishment for me.

A counselor at school talked to me after I broke my cousin's nose. She told me not to feel guilty about Theresa's death because it was an accident. Not feel guilty? I've lived with guilt almost my whole life. She also suggested I not break any more noses, which she didn't imagine was an accident. She told me I could talk to her if I needed to, and I did a few times. Probably the best thing she did for me was to encourage me to write again; she helped me get a job with the school newspaper.

At a Christmas gathering about three years ago, my mother started telling the same story about how if I had just watched Theresa more carefully, she'd still be alive. I screamed at my mother, "Who left out the hot water, anyway? Not me." I had just finally had it. I left and went out into the cold. I felt a warm arm around me. It was Mark. He smiled and put his other hand to his nose. He asked me, "Wanna punch me again?" But this time he was compassionate.

Mark and I went back into the house and sat in the den together. I cried some for all those years I felt lonely, guilty, and frustrated. He apologized to me for what he had said so long ago. We talked and talked about Theresa's death, and I felt some kind of . . . I don't know . . . peace, I guess, inside. I told Mark it was the best present anyone ever gave me. We've stayed close ever since.

I sat down and talked with my mother about Theresa's death about six months ago. It wasn't easy. We both would rather have blamed each other than have taken responsibility for such an awful death. But while we blamed each other outwardly, inside we both had huge globs of guilt.

My dad and I never really did get along after Theresa's death. He just seemed to work more, and I worked harder at not seeing him or talking to him. Even though he died five years ago, I feel like he died a long time ago in my life. I didn't want the same thing to happen with my mother and me. We still aren't completely reconciled, but we've started going to a grief group together. It's helping us both.

I'm learning to take care of my feelings about Theresa's death. I had filled the void I felt by either blaming myself or keeping busy taking care of other people's feelings. It's way past time for me to get on with my life. Still, if I'm honest, I have those times when I feel I would give almost anything to have those two minutes back.

I Was Only Good for Death

George

George, thirty-four, has had a rugged trip through grief. His mother, diagnosed paranoid schizophrenic, committed suicide when he was fifteen years old. He was encouraged to keep the suicide a secret and, as a result, has worked very hard to come to grips with his mother's death. He feels and thinks deeply, speaks honestly, and is determined to heal.

I learned about George's story briefly one morning at 4:30 over coffee. We spoke often of him being willing to tell his story and tried for four months to set an appointment. Finally, one Sunday afternoon, a most pensive young man sat at my kitchen table telling the following story. Throughout the interview George remained amazingly calm, stroking his beard as he spoke.

To watch someone like George begin healing from grief and enter

135

again into the mainstream of life is pure gold. To receive a phone call the next day from George thanking me for listening to his story was a mutual honor.

I didn't really grieve her death at the time. Maybe I had learned too well to deal with loss. She was paranoid schizophrenic, and she had been suicidal before my sister and I were even born. I heard her threaten suicide so many times that I guess I was just numb to the threats. And as a family, we were always dealing with loss in terms of her illness. She would frequently disappear for months at a time. She was also hospitalized several times while I was growing up. I grieved most of my life before her death, because I could not count on her being available.

My sister is two years older than I am. By the time my mom did kill herself, my sister and I were already survivors, taking care of ourselves. We had a lot of independence. When you can't count on parents, you learn early to count on yourself. My dad was always taking care of Mom, and Mom didn't take care of us, so we did.

I had a sense of relief when she died. She had suffered so much. And she was always doing these crazy things—I was glad that was over with and I wouldn't have to deal with her craziness anymore.

Before she died I was dealing with my own problems of finding meaning. I was preoccupied with it, and I guess her illness and her death added further to my sense of meaninglessness about life.

About two months after her death I remember actually beginning to feel something about her suicide. I was over at my friend Dave's house. We were down in his basement. His mom was there and she asked how I was doing, and how my dad and my sister were doing. I said, "Fine." She said, "Well, is your sister doing any of the cooking now that your mother is gone?" And it hit me. I just got this really heavy feeling in my stomach and became real sad. It was really the first time I actually felt anything about my mom not being around. That was the first time I remember feeling anything at all about her death. It was a very deep feeling of heaviness and sadness.

About a year after that I remember feeling that heaviness again. I was listening to music. It was kind of a wintry day, sunny outside, but I was feeling this heavy melancholy. I thought about death and her suicide, and for a long time after that I would feel that melancholy at funerals.

I went to a lot of funerals the year after my mom died. It may sound morbid, but I found a comfort in the melancholy. In my searching for meaning to life, I found solace in this feeling of melancholy. There was a place inside me for this feeling; it was *my* feeling. I felt it somehow meant there was a place for me in life. At funerals I assumed other people facing loss were going through the same thing I was going through. It would be years before I realized people handled grief differently.

When you are grieving, it helps to name your pain. *Suicide* was such a shameful word that I didn't have that chance. The whole thing was supposed to be a secret. The Catholic church was just starting to open its cemeteries to people who had committed suicide. My dad told my sister and me that we weren't supposed to tell anybody how she died. I started hearing rumors that she overdosed on drugs. We were supposed to say she had died of cancer or a heart attack. I know schizophrenia now is considered a physical problem as well as a mental disorder, but as sick as my mom was mentally, she was really physically very healthy. She didn't have cancer; she didn't have heart trouble. She jumped out of a twelve-story building.

There wasn't any dialogue at home. My dad didn't talk about her death and didn't want us to talk about it. My dad just worked a lot. One day he said, "I have to be both a mother and a father to you." But he wasn't open to any "normal" conversation like, "How are you doing?" He just worked two jobs. It was like he was more damaged than my sister and I were. I mostly dealt with questions like, "How come life doesn't make any sense to me?" on my own. We didn't even discuss basic social things, like dating etiquette.

After my mom died, I started looking for another mother. I wanted a mom who would be around and be there for me.

I used to work at a laundromat. As I would walk to work, I would pass this one place that had some sort of exhaust fan blowing. When I walked past, I would smell drying clothes and fabric softener, and that always brought on a feeling of wanting another mother who was very domestic. That was my concept of motherhood. I would hope, like on the "Brady Bunch" or like in a goofy movie where two people who were widowed with lots of kids got married, that my dad would meet and marry a great mom. That never happened. Soon I realized my dating choices were based on seeking mothering.

As I tried to deal with my mom's suicide, I found a lot of people couldn't deal with it. I didn't tell anyone what happened to my mom until almost a year after she died. I went to a Catholic high school, and during homeroom our school would have announcements. If someone had a death in the family they would ask you to pray for the soul of the person, who usually was the father or mother of some student. In my case, my mom died over the summer, so there wasn't that opportunity.

When I got back to school, no one knew about my mom's suicide or said anything except for one teacher. He said, "I am really sorry to hear about your mom. If I can be of any help, let me know." I was shocked. I thought my mom's death was a secret. I wasn't ready to receive that kind of help.

In my junior year—two years after my mother died—I had a morality class. One of the topics we dealt with was death. I remember the teacher saying that death is a victory, and that the proper response to death is ultimately joy because the person who died has gone to heaven and is with God again. I remember feeling rage and shame at hearing that. The response didn't deal with my reality. Suicide is a very shameful thing.

I remember asking the teacher, "What about people who commit suicide? If somebody is murdered, he is a victim. God has mercy on victims. If someone dies of a disease, that is an understandable tragedy. But when someone jumps out of a twelve-story building, what can you do with that?" He said, "I don't know."

I didn't talk about my mom's death with any of the guidance counselors or anyone at school until my senior year. I told my guidance counselor, and he gave me a list of books to read about death. I didn't, because I didn't see how that was going to help me.

It was like flying blind for a long time. Something was eating me up inside and took a lot of energy. I really didn't have a clue or any balance as to what I needed to be doing in day-to-day life. I carried my grief inside.

I went to college and flunked out after my first quarter because I was just so depressed. Nothing held meaning for me.

Because I was so used to our family keeping secrets, I told my dad I dropped out of school rather than telling the truth.

Now I had some free time. One of the things I was asked to do during this time was to sit with an uncle of mine who was dying of cancer. He was also an alcoholic. The doctors couldn't do anything for him because the cancer had spread too far by the time they found it. So, I would go over and sit with him during the day and watch soap operas. Basically, I watched him die. And I simply thought, "This is what life is about."

When I looked at other friends of mine who were going to college, or moving some other way into life, it seemed I was moving into death. I was around all these sick, dying people, and I felt totally overwhelmed. I couldn't talk about it with anyone. I just seemed to keep getting hit by death.

For my uncle's funeral, I drove a lot of people around. I took my aunt around to take care of things, picked up people at the airport, ran errands. I felt useful. I started to become very comfortable with wakes and funerals.

Grief was cutting into my social development even more now. I felt I was only good for death, and that was it. I felt an inevitability; there was no way of escaping death.

I didn't visit my mother's grave until four years after her death. It was late winter and I was visiting a friend who lived near the cemetery. I walked home, which was a good four to five-mile walk, and I decided to go through the cemetery. I found her grave and just stood there. It was pretty weird seeing her name on the headstone. Then I noticed they got the date of death wrong. They gave her three more days than she had actually lived. In our family, we have a history of not doing things quite right; it seems like that went all the way to the grave with my mom.

I Was Only Good for Death – George

I didn't know what to expect at the cemetery. I remember feeling real sad. It was a very heavy sadness, like a longing because I felt no roots, no dock. That feeling would be recurrent for several years. At the same time, those moments were some of the more honest times I ever spent with my mom or her memory in my life.

My mom's illness had meant that the family revolved around her. If she disappeared to California for three months, or if the police called from another state, she was the focus of the family—and she was pretty much helpless.

My sister wouldn't or couldn't accept that helplessness. She said things like, "This is nonsense. She's supposed to be doing certain things, and she's not," or "I'm not going to buy this cop-out." I remember thinking my sister had a lot of guts to say those things, because I was just overwhelmed with self-pity or whatever.

The fact that my sister didn't buy into making excuses all the time helped her a lot. She didn't get bogged down in feelings like I did. She dealt with her own feelings, but she wasn't immobilized by the situation like I was. I wish I could have felt the way my sister did.

About twelve years ago I became preoccupied with the fact that everything ended. Whatever the situation—work, friendships, relationships, groups—I kept feeling *This will end sometime*. I couldn't just enjoy an experience or encounter for what it was worth at the time. I knew I would be without it someday.

This reaction went too far, and it was devastating. Showing up for work every day or being on time for an appointment—I couldn't make that much commitment to life. Then I started looking for escapes to dull my pain. Drinking was one. Sex was another. When I was twenty-five or so, I realized that my way of dealing with life wasn't working.

I went to Alcoholics Anonymous and started to get into recovery. Through the program, bit by bit, I learned to parent myself. And, bit by bit, I allowed myself to be parented by some of the other people in recovery.

Later that same year I joined a group for sex addiction. That was closer to being the core issue for me. I had to give up that behavior before I could get to anything else.

I did finally get to the place where I realized and acknowledged I was grieving the loss of my mother. That was September 1991. I went to a day of recollection at church, and there was a priest who was talking about his brother who had committed suicide. When he talked about his brother's death, I just lost it. All of the old feelings came back. I was totally, completely overwhelmed with sadness, and I just wanted to cry. One of my mom's friends was there, and every time I looked at her I thought of my mom. It was rough to even look her in the eye.

That experience was a breakthrough for me, though, because I now knew what was happening. I was finally at a place where I knew, "I am starting to grieve my mother's death. I'm finally letting it happen." Then I called a friend from AA whose sister had committed suicide, and we talked about it some. I got books on grief, suicide, and mental illness.

I started going to a support meeting for family members of people who had committed suicide, and I found some books very helpful. There was really nothing to do other than feel the grief and talk about it. It was painful, really painful. I didn't like feeling the sadness and loss. But I found that, as you go through the sadness and pain, they pass.

For the first time in my life, I can see and feel the benefit of going through my life experiences and going through grief. I realize that there was something good there. It's like the analogy that plants don't grow unless you throw crap on them. That was true for me. There was this big compost heap sitting on the top of my soul for all these years, and I actually was starting to grow because of it.

Growth is ongoing, though. Many books say it takes about two years to grieve a big loss like a death. That's assuming you let it happen. For me, letting grief happen took about fifteen years.

Shortly after telling me his story, George called his sister and read her the story you have just read. Then he called me and told me that it was freeing and healing for both of them to have him tell his story, and for them to be able to reaffirm each other's reality of their mother's life and death.

Six months later, George flew from Chicago to Texas and spent Christmas with his sister. It was the first Christmas they had spent together in fourteen years—since his sister left home after their mother's suicide.

This is the kind of surprise hope I see as people tell their stories and move into acceptance.

I Climbed a Mountain!
Edythe

This interview was with a seventy-five-year-old woman six months after her husband of fifty-eight years died. At the time of the interview, she herself had been diagnosed with leukemia and had lived two years longer than doctors had expected. Her last words to me were, "Get this story right. I may well be dead myself by the time it is in print." And then she smiled broadly.

My son died at thirty when his car rolled over, killing him as he tried to avoid a deer that had jumped into his path. When a child dies like that, you mourn the lost possibilities for his life as much as his death.

One of our daughters was widowed twice within ten years and was left with three young children. My husband and I knew deep grief when we watched helplessly as several of our grandchildren fought alcoholism.

Grief was no stranger to my life. It would seem that after several grief experiences I would have built a reservoir of skills or an expertise in weaving the threads of loss and pain into the fabric of life and "get on with it." That doesn't seem to happen. At least not to me. Nor can family, friends, or trained personnel mitigate the suffering.

I discovered that accepting my own responsibility for doing the work of coping with grief—and it is work!—is the toughest step in the grief process.

My husband's death was no surprise. Francis had been diagnosed diabetic twenty years before he died. His compliance with diabetes maintenance and the advice of his physician was less than half-hearted. Fran knew of the diabetes ten years before his retirement. His work as a pastor was at a crucial stage. I believe he chose to make few changes in his lifestyle so he could handle the work he felt called as a minister to do.

Both of our daughters have nursing degrees. They suggested repeatedly that he give more attention to his health. His neglect of his physical health gave all of us pain after his death. Were we guilty of going along with his choices because we understood how he felt about his work? Or, were we not secretly proud that he chose to go on as he did, rather than give up for the sake of a few more months of life?

I personally harbor guilt because it was easier to do as he asked than to insist he live as others suggested. I have had to accept that this is a harsh reality I will have to live with. It is impossible to make changes at this point. That's just the way it is.

For thirty years, Fran had been the pastor of a large congregation of German families living in a small community. The families built a large stone church. But those families prospered and moved into the suburbs. They joined other churches.

The original church was now in a busy inner-city commercial area where very few people resided. The town rapidly became a city and it was impossible for the few, mostly elderly members to support the 175-year-old building.

The church was headed for extinction. It was a period of great emotional stress for the remaining members. Also former members had deep emotional ties to the church where they were raised and married and had their children baptized. Fran tried vainly to prevent the closing of the church.

My husband had emotional ties not only to the congregation, but to the community in which the church was located. I believe that the emotional stress of those last ten years of his ministry were full of change that accelerated his decline. His health deteriorated to the point where he could not take part in the closing worship service. He had to be hospitalized with stress-related illness.

He lived quietly in retirement for ten more years. We bought a home thirty miles away from the parish, close to one of our daughters. Almost immediately he was hospitalized, and within a year he had undergone his first of seven amputations. His health problems made him more dependent on me and others.

We were grateful that the home we had bought provided the facilities for his care and comfort. Throughout his entire life he had enjoyed fine music and he played it night and day. Visits by members of former congregations and frequent drop-ins by children and grandchildren rounded out his days.

He was also able to baptize his first great-grandchild.

With Those Who Grieve

∾

Arrangements were made with the pastor of a nearby congregation. After enough logistical planning to move an army and with the help of many strong arms, this pastor/great-grandfather was carried into the church to perform his last pastoral act. From his wheelchair he baptized his great-granddaughter. This was a precious moment for him and a happy memory for all of us.

His final forty-five days were spent in intensive care. He had begged us not to let him die in the hospital, but it was impossible to give him the health care he needed at home. Family members were with him most of his waking hours. When life-support systems were removed a few days before he died, he could not speak. He seemed to have something very important he wanted to say to me, but could not form the words. For many, many nights after he died as I tried to sleep I heard over and over the unintelligible sounds he had made. Then I realized he was saying, "I love you, I love you, I love you."

On his final day he seemed lethargic but peaceful. He gave us feeble smiles. He died in my arms. I felt an overwhelming peace and gratitude that his suffering had ended. That feeling carried me through the funeral and burial. I had been praying for weeks that he would be released from his suffering and now he was. I was strengthened by the faith my husband and I had shared and by the love and support of our daughters who were grieving the loss of their father.

I came home alone to the house we had shared. Here I felt my husband's presence. I listened to his music and imagined him sitting there in his wheelchair. I wore his old sweaters imagining I could feel his arms around me. When I needed to make a decision, I was sure I knew exactly what his advice would be. After all, I had spent fifty-eight years listening to his advice and opinions!

I Climbed a Mountain! – Edythe

While all of this was comforting, I began to realize this was not the real world. My husband's care had absorbed most of my time. Now there was too much empty time. For a long time I had been unable to leave him alone except for brief excursions to my doctor's office or to the grocery store. Now friends invited me out. The whole time I'd be out, I kept feeling that I needed to get home to take care of Fran. I think I was being forced to face reality, but something within me wanted to resist. Why couldn't I go on as I had, feeling his presence although he was not physically there?

From the moment we had met we shared a deep faith. That faith had been the strongest bond of our marriage. Our shared faith kept us together when human frailties and desires might have proven otherwise. After our children were grown, my own job had meant that we were separated geographically for short periods of time, but we never doubted that each was behind the other. What had changed?

In the worship service of our denomination we acknowledge that the heavenly beings and the earthbound saints work together praising the Lord. Now each time I worshiped I was eager to get to the reassurance of those words in the service, feeling a spiritual comfort and bond with Fran.

On All Saints Day, our congregation reads the names of members who have died in the preceding year and places roses on the altar in their memory.

As I heard Fran's name read aloud, I knew I could no longer live in the false world I had created. I was trying to be the same person I was just moments before his death. That person no longer existed. Those ties were severed and the realization was frightening. If I wasn't that person, who was I?

With Those Who Grieve

∞

The work of coping with grief took on a new dimension. During his retirement, my husband and I had time to discuss many things. We had talked about our finances and how they might be handled in the event of the death of either of us. We talked of what income we might expect and what kind of legal and financial responsibilities might fall to a survivor. We discussed our funeral and burial arrangements.

These discussions made it much easier to carry out these responsibilities. So many people feel it is too emotional or too morbid to discuss one's own death, but I'm thankful we did. However, there are many topics we did not consider, which I wish now we had talked about. Chief among these is the question, "What happens to the relationship that has existed between husband and wife?" It is certainly different after death, but it is not canceled out and forgotten. Maybe I feel this way because I am still reluctant to let go.

It was our relationship that was so important in shaping me into the person I am. It is as though we traveled together until we came to a crossing, one road marked for me and the other for him. We are no longer on the same road, but I will be forever influenced by the impact of that first part of the journey. I know that decisions I make will bear the marks of that relationship.

I am an inveterate list maker, and I decided I ought to get some things on paper before setting out to build a new life. What might I enjoy doing? How could I contribute to others' lives? I decided I most enjoyed finding opportunities to satisfy my curiosity about people, what they do and how they live, more about the history of peoples beyond my own nation, and I wanted more hands-on experience to supplement my reading.

With that list made, I wrote down what I had to bring to

these pursuits: talents, education, experience, and so on. I became uncomfortable making these lists. Planning a life was an occupation for high school students. Then I remembered I have less time ahead and felt it imperative to keep on.

Several things helped give me courage to keep on. I was invited by the chaplains' organization of the hospital in which my husband died to speak to their monthly meeting on new opportunities for women. Women in general, not only women chaplains. I had been involved in women's issues educationally and professionally. Here was a real challenge to update my own information and to inform others.

Ninety percent of the audience was male. I found them astonishingly receptive. They asked many questions and requested sources they might read for further information on the subject. The older chaplains were even more interested than the younger ones. I had expected the younger chaplains to have greater exposure to the issue. This project gave a great boost to my self-esteem.

And then there was my summer vacation. My daughter, son-in-law, and their two teenagers have enjoyed several summer vacations at Acadia National Park in Maine. They planned a vacation the summer after my husband's death. "Come, relax with us," invited my daughter. "Come, climb a mountain with us," urged the teenagers. I said, "I'm old. I can't see."

I went with them, planning to occupy myself on terra firma while they climbed. They had other ideas. With my grandson in front holding out a steady arm, and my son-in-law behind pushing and shoving, I climbed a mountain! At seventy-five, I climbed a mountain and found a new me. I could try new things in my life.

I volunteered to serve as a teacher's aide for three sixth grade classes in a rural elementary school and discovered new facets of myself. I discovered a whole new generation of young people—curious, noisy, combative, but concerned about the earth, their futures, and their classmates. When I was forced to take time off for illness, they designed get-well cards in their computer courses. I looked for jokes and puzzles to intrigue them and they found jokes to tease me. Being accepted in a world so different from my own has taught me much about being flexible.

Who am I? I am not alone. I am not afraid. I am not without hope. The answers are coming. I am a person with a history to tell, with hopes and abilities and great resources. I am traveling a new trail and I am not sure where I am heading, but I am not alone. Not feeling alone is important to me. I enjoy times of solitude, and I enjoy equally well times spent with family, friends, and with new acquaintances. I try to remember that keeping relationships vital requires initiation and opening up on my part as well as responding to the efforts of others.

Of great importance to me in the work of handling grief is the loving support of family. Our struggle to overcome our common loss is starting to be replaced by happiness as we remember together Fran's impact on our lives. We can tell our stories over and over as the young ones grow and ask for stories. We ignore death as a dividing line between "then, when he was alive" and "now, when he lives in pictures and memories." We guard zealously family rituals that help us recall the legacy, not with the pain of his death, but with gratitude for his life, whose essence lives on within us.

Healing Does Happen, But Wounds Remain
Carl

Carl, forty-four, is a minister in Pennsylvania. His father died ten years ago. Even so, the pain of recounting the loss of his father is so deep, that this interview was done in two parts, allowing Carl time to continue healing in his grieving process.

My wife Cindy, my mother, and I had a great visit with Father the evening before he died. He was again in the Reading Hospital and Medical Center, and that was good news. His return to the hospital meant that he was back on track for heart bypass surgery after a delay of over a month.

Father had known for several years that he had heart trouble. It was the common problem of blocked arteries causing angina pain. A few years earlier, a doctor at another hospital had

153

informed Father that he should have surgery, but Father wasn't ready. An increase in his level of discomfort coupled with the success that his oldest brother had with a similar operation now led him to consent to surgery.

So in April 1983 he entered the hospital. Initial testing was done, including heart catheterization. The doctors consulted with one another. In a conversation that Father could overhear from his hospital bed, an insensitive doctor told the surgeon, "You've got quite a challenge here." Blood vessels were bad in more places than in the heart.

Father continued to stay in the hospital and was only two days away from surgery when the doctors decided to postpone the operation. There were no veins in his legs suitable to use in bypasses. So the doctors decided to try something new: They would connect an artery to a vein in the arm, thereby enlarging the vein. Once the vein was strong and large enough, the surgery would be rescheduled.

We waited another month, and Father seemed weaker. "Before going to the hospital I could walk two miles," he said. "Now I can hardly walk two blocks." We knew that his condition was serious, and we wanted the operation completed. Finally the surgeon said that Father was ready.

I had driven up from Philadelphia to the Reading Hospital and Medical Center to visit him, along with my wife and my mother. He explained something about plumbing. He joked about my leaving early to vote. When I did leave Father, Mother, and Cindy about 7:30 P.M., Father seemed in good spirits. The operation was scheduled for Thursday.

It was not to be. Wednesday morning at six o'clock we received a call. I felt worried as soon as I heard the ring. A doctor asked for my mother, who was staying with us in our home near Reading. We should come to the hospital, he said; Father had a problem during the night. My first thought was, "Not another delay." Then I expected something even worse. I couldn't drive and asked Cindy to. On the way, Mother said, "Pray, Carl." I felt it was too late.

When we arrived at the hospital, a doctor met us. Father was dead. About 3:00 A.M. nurses found that he didn't have a pulse—no one knew how long he had been that way. They tried to restart his heart and even considered performing the scheduled surgery immediately. But his heartbeat could not be sustained. There was no way of knowing how long his brain had been without oxygen. The doctor took us to the body. I was upset but able to function.

I called Sally, my sister. A call to Mother's brother, Ambrose, told him and his sister, Carrie, that Father was dead. We waited at the hospital until Sally came. "Damn" was her first word.

After spending time with Sally at the hospital—I can't remember how long—Mother, Cindy, and I returned to my house to get our belongings. Then we drove the fifty miles to Mother's house in Valley View. At that point I felt cheated: I had looked forward to having Mother and Father stay with us during the first week or so of his recovery. Now we wouldn't have that time together.

The next days are a blur. I remember our family sitting together and crying. I also can remember some specific incidents, including a visit by two of my sister's friends, who brought a roast turkey. Father's brothers, James and Ralph, came for a brief visit.

The pastor came to plan the funeral; I read to him parts of a sermon that I had given once, "Blanks, Gaps, and Voids," and suggested that it might have themes appropriate for the funeral.

I remember, too, going to Aunt Carrie's house for many meals; we were too numb to cook and not very hungry. It seemed as if life was going on around us but that we were in suspension. That is, usually I feel as if I am in control of my life and many of the events around me. Now it seemed as if I was passive and had to let the world go along by itself. I could not be in control.

I remember that we said "I love you" constantly—as if Mother, Sally, Cindy, and I were trying to assure each other of our affection in case yet another of us should disappear. We thought of possible arrangements for the future; I read an introduction to one of Father's carpentry books and was moved by a quote about a house, taking this to be a sign that we should certainly hold onto his house and, for weekends at least, move in with Mother.

Then, too, there were funeral arrangements to be made. We wanted a viewing only for the immediate family and for Father's and Mother's brothers and sisters. After that, the body would be cremated. The family would bury the ashes, then hold a memorial service.

The viewing was OK. Father's face was puffier than usual, though the profile looked like him. What I remember best is the end of the viewing, when most of the people had left and our immediate family sat alone with Father's body. I took a sample of hair—It seems very Victorian now, but it was important at the time, even though it also seemed disrespectful.

The memorial service was fine. I read a Bible passage. After the service I helped greet the people who attended. I was told that I seemed composed, and I do believe that I took everything well except the reading was difficult. It was a somewhat formal setting in which we repeated the story of Father's death over and over again. I could tell the story without tears, but I couldn't really focus my thoughts on Father himself without breaking down. So I controlled my thoughts and did OK.

After the service and some time with the family, I headed back to our apartment in Philadelphia. Cindy stayed with Mother, but I was scheduled to take part in a meeting the next day and felt that duty called. The people at the meeting were supportive, and it went OK. Now the crying came at times when I was alone.

A coworker, Ray, said that if I wanted to talk, he would listen; when his parents died, he found that he wanted to talk about them. Another coworker, Bob, said that although he had lost neither father nor wife, he thought that losing a father would be rougher because of the formative, foundational role a father plays in a life. I appreciated knowing that other people also valued their fathers; it let me know that they appreciated the fact that I had lost something that could never be replaced.

For the next year I found it difficult to talk in-depth to Mother about Father without becoming teary. Even now, ten years later, if I really focus my thoughts on Father I can still become very sad.

After completing this part of the interview, Carl needed to stop. It would be months before we met again.

Although Father was gone from us we believed that all was well with him. Our faith tells us that. Then, too, we took comfort in some "signs." For example, one day when I was in Philadelphia,

Mother and Cindy were together in the garden near an iris bed in which Father had worked—he had always been the outside person, taking care of the flowers. One pure white iris was blooming. When they saw that iris, both Mother and Cindy had the same immediate thought: it's a sign that Father is all right. When they told me that story, and two others concerning experiences that Mother had, I felt more content too.

We recognized, though, that our lives would never be the same again. A gap remains. I sense it not only at such times as holidays, but also when I am involved in building something. Father was good with tools and working around a house. So when we built a house next to Mother's, I often thought about him and what he would say or do.

In fact, the work area in Father's basement seemed to be the part of the house most uniquely his. That is where his power saw, workbench, other tools, and fishing gear were kept. There was a folding chair, for example, on which he had placed some clothing and a hat; for a long time I did not want Mother to move anything from that chair. It was a still-life created by him, representing him.

Now the chair has been moved, the clothing dispersed. This year I took the power saw from the basement and moved it to my new garage; we are also planning to move the workbench. I must say, though, that the thought of moving the workbench causes me some uneasiness. With the moving of his bench and tools, the part of the house most uniquely Father's will be stripped of his touch. It is as if we are removing yet another part of him. On the other hand, his bench will be more a part of my daily life.

Because we now live in a new house next to my mother, and because Cindy's parents are still both alive, Father's absence is very obvious. The awareness of that absence no longer causes me great sorrow; we learn to get on with our lives. But I believe that I do keep myself slightly distant from Father in order to avoid a more acute pain. For example, I have a recording of an interview I did with him about his life; although I treasure having the recording, I have never listened to it since his death and do not really want to now. If we had a transcription of the tape, I think I could read it without difficulty. I am not yet ready to hear Father's voice again.

Many events can bring Father and his death to mind: the death of someone else's father, my building something, seeing his picture in our living room, visiting one of his surviving siblings, and so forth. So healing takes place, but wounds remain. I consider the death of my father to be the worst experience of my life. If I could undo any one thing from my past, that would be it.

Who Will Value My Tears?
Charlene

Charlene's story of surviving grief was told to me through a series of visits.

She was married to her husband, Clarence, in 1958. Early in their marriage, Charlene miscarried. Later they had a daughter, Deborah, who died in childhood. Throughout their marriage, she kept a series of seven journals and made entries nearly every day. They now sit on the coffee table in her living room.

After Clarence's death in 1978, she continued her practice of keeping a journal, though not on a daily basis. She told part of her story to me through her journal entries, which honestly chronicle joys, pains, special events, and everyday happenings during her marriage. Her journals also helped her through her grieving process, which she says "gets easier but is never really done. I still miss him deeply; some days are harder than other days."

With Those Who Grieve

Charlene says that during the hard and sad times since Clarence's death, she finds comfort in reading through her journals. "I couldn't look at my writings I had done until almost a year after Clarence died. Now, however, if I feel really blue or down, I'll pick up one of my books and read what I wrote."

What she finds especially hard is the occasional loneliness of living alone. "We did so much as a couple . . . traveled, fought, did little favors for each other, celebrated, got on each other's nerves, and grieved. Living alone I find I can distort our marriage. I can think it was always filled with beautiful, wonderful, happy times. Our marriage was a good one, but it wasn't just the romantic and happy times. I can forget that. So, often—especially in the middle of the night—I read through one of my journals."

Char says that her journals help her remember her marriage more realistically, and that has helped her as she has grieved. "I guess I get a sense of balance and peace from reading what happened years ago. I'm not sure how or why, but reading what I wrote brings me out of depression or feeling sorry for myself. Sometimes I can laugh at something that seemed devastating at the time. Sometimes I shed some tears. I feel like Clarence is with me when I read them.

"I found that I miss the fights as well as the times we made up. Most of all, I found that it's the everyday things, the mundane things that you miss most. Maybe that's really what life is; you just don't know it at the time."

Here, then, is a part of Charlene's story told through some of her journal entries and some comments about conversations between us. Her pet names for Clarence were "C.," "Clare," and "Buttons." Any bracketed material is for the reader's clarification. Everything else tells Charlene's story for her.

Who Will Value My Tears? – Charlene

∞

Our Wedding Day, August 16, 1958

Clare gave me this sketchbook as a wedding gift. He says he never wants me to give up my art because it means so much to me. I think I'll draw and write in it about our first year of marriage. He feels badly we couldn't have a big church wedding. But we knew our religious differences would mean that. It doesn't matter that we had a simple ceremony. Our family and a few friends could be there. Plus we didn't have the money. I'd rather spend our money on this apartment in the city. I'm finishing a painting of myself to give him, but I can't get it just right.

September 1, 1958

Now that I am back at work, it seems so strange to be called "Mrs. D—" rather than "Miss T—" [names withheld at Charlene's request]. When I get home to our apartment, though, it seems like I've been Mrs. Clarence D— for a long time. I like coming home to someone else and decorating our place together.

October 16, 1958

C. brought me a beautiful rose today to celebrate our being married two months. I fixed a special dinner.

Thanksgiving, 1958

Our first holiday together! I was so nervous having my family and his family together. His mother still makes it clear that she doesn't think I'm good enough for her son. That hurts and makes me mad. Our parents are still fighting religion. Money seems to be a bigger problem. We save for a house, and there is little extra money. Next year someone else can fix the turkey!

With Those Who Grieve

∞

Our First Christmas, 1958

We had a quiet, nice Christmas. Last year C. lavished me with gifts. But now we have a tighter budget (and do we fight!). I got a set of drawing pencils from C. and a beautiful white sweater I can wear to work. I gave C. the self-portrait I finally finished and framed. He said he will take it to work with him. I told him that I still didn't have it right, and he said, "It's fine. You're cute as a button." I decided to start calling him Mr. Buttons. He thought it was funny.

I was so glad C. would go to midnight Mass with me. That may have been the best present of all. We bought a cute little tree, and I made a lot of the decorations for it. I decorated one red shiny one for C. with our wedding date and two hearts on it. I think he liked that the best of all. He said we will put it on our tree every year until we are too old to hang it anymore.

New Year's Day, 1959

C. surprised me by taking me out on the town last night. I wondered if we could afford it, but C. said he had saved a few dollars each week since we were married for a special occasion. We talked about having children, and decided to have a baby this year and wait for the house. We took down the Christmas tree and C. said, "Next year Santa will have to visit and bring the baby a very special present." I didn't know he could get so excited about a baby! I know this child will have lots of love.

January 23, 1959

I'm sick of winter. Everything seems so gray. Even C. seems to be drab. Maybe we should postpone a baby.

Who Will Value My Tears? – Charlene

February 1, 1959

I'm not sure, but I think it's too late to postpone the baby. I'll see Dr. Wilson next week and see. I'm excited. Confused. Worried. Thrilled. I want to give this news to C. for a Valentine's gift. I don't know if I can really tell if I'm pregnant, but I feel like someone tiny is inside there.

February 10, 1959

I'm pregnant! I don't know if I can keep it a secret until Valentine's Day!

February 14, 1959

I gave Buttons a Valentine with a big heart on the front that I made. On the inside I wrote, "Will you be our Valentine? Love, Char and Baby." He cried and laughed and shook his head all night. We'll be a family of our own in time for the holidays.

February 15, 1959

C. gave me a baby blanket for my birthday present. All day he called every chance he got. I don't think we can believe it yet. Ruth [mother-in-law] sent me a nice card for my birthday. Maybe she'll like being a grandmother!

February 28, 1959

We decided to pick out names for the baby. If it's a girl, it will be Elizabeth; if it's a boy, Edward. Nice and royal. C. wants to get a house now more than before. I don't know how we can afford both a new baby and a house. Plus I won't be working soon. C. says I shouldn't worry. But I do worry.

March 18, 1959

This is the saddest day of my life. I miscarried. All our baby dreams gone.

March 21, 1959

Why do people avoid me or whisper around me? Isn't there anyone to talk to that knows this awful pain? I can't be the only woman to ever miscarry, but I'm starting to feel that way. Dr. Wilson told me to rest, come back to see him, and C. and I could "try again in no time." I feel like dying, not like giving birth.

This was as far as we read my first visit. Char and I had tea afterward and she spoke of the loss of miscarriage. She said she wished she could have talked to even one other woman who could understand her pain. She pointed out that grief groups were not really in existence at the time she miscarried.

Both she and Clarence were at a loss to talk about the miscarriage for several years. "It was just assumed," Char said, "that after physically healing, we'd try to have children again right away. But what about our hopes, our dreams, our grief? One nurse spent about fifteen minutes with me. Then, it was like life just went on as if nothing happened."

On my second visit, Char was far more at ease with me. She had marked several journal entries for me in her second journal. Since much was repetitive, we agreed together on sharing the following entries.

June 24, 1960

It feels so wonderful to own our own home. (Actually the bank owns most of it.) But we know we can pay it off brick by brick.

It's small and cozy. Just right for Buttons, me, Tex [their dog], and hopefully a baby in another year. We'll have to do a lot of decorating, but it gives my art an outlet.

July 4, 1960
I don't understand how holidays can become times to fight so much over nothing. The day was going fine until I realized we had no dog food. I swear we fought for an hour over dog food.

August 29, 1960
I think I'm pregnant again. I got out the baby blanket C. gave me before. I washed it and it smelled so clean and wonderful I just buried my face in it and cried.

October 3, 1960
I'll have to quit work now that I'm pregnant. Less money, but more time to get ready for the baby. C. says he expects a raise in December, so "he'll make the money and I'll make the baby."

December 14, 1960
The doctor says I need to spend more time in bed. I'll do it to keep the baby healthy. We figure I got pregnant the beginning of July . . . maybe after that fight about dog food! I'm NOT calling the baby TEX!!

Christmas, 1960
The whole Christmas story seems more real to me now with the baby on the way. I am getting impatient and uncomfortable. C. got a raise and a big Christmas bonus. We're going to buy things for the baby with the bonus.

With Those Who Grieve

February 2, 1961

Our furnace broke. At first I cried because we had to get a new furnace with the bonus C. got. But he laughed and said, "Well, the baby will have to be warm, too."

February 14, 1961

C. is less romantic. I know he is doing things around the house for the baby, but I don't like feeling like I get his leftover love. Maybe it's me. One day up; one day down. Usually up and down in the same day.

March 11, 1961

Our Deborah. Our baby. Either she or the doctor didn't have the date right. I don't think I've ever seen anything or anyone so beautiful. I want to try to remember her just like this so I can do a sketch. I don't think I'll draw about labor!

March 14, 1961

The doctor is worried about me. I feel fine, but he says I've been bleeding since the delivery. C. is worried. Tomorrow another doctor sees me.

April 16, 1961

This is NOT how I planned. I have a baby; I lose a uterus. Of course I want Deborah. But can no one understand I also lost a part, a precious part, of me?

C. tries to cheer me. My mother tries to comfort me. C.'s mother scolds me for not being happier with Deborah. I AM HAPPY WITH DEBORAH. I just. . . .

Who Will Value My Tears? – Charlene

∞

Christmas, 1961
What fun! Deborah watches and watches the lights on the tree. Tex and she are best of friends. C. is so good with her. All the relatives running around scared Deborah. She screamed and screamed. I wish I could be as free to scream and squeal with delight like her.

March 11, 1962
Deborah—one year old! It seems like she just was born, and yet like she's been with us forever. I have a hard time remembering what it was like with just C. and me. Except quieter. Definitely quieter.

August 3, 1962
C. has a new job offer. It would mean better opportunities for him and probably more financial security. But, we would have to move away from here. Away from our home. Away from our friends and family. *Away.* I hate that word today.

October 15, 1962
Friends had a farewell party for us. I cried and cried. I told C. he and Tex could move and Deborah and I would stay here. I just don't want to lose anything else.

February 24, 1963
Deborah is in the hospital. She is running a temperature of 105 degrees, but the doctors say that children do that often. Her body looks so tiny. I sit by her bed as long as they'll let me. And pray.

February 27, 1963
Deborah died.

With Those Who Grieve

∽

March 1, 1963

Clare and I don't know what to say to each other. Friends don't know. The priest doesn't know. Does God know?

May 4, 1963

C. and I avoid each other. I sit in the nursery and rock for hours without knowing. My mother said the best thing is "to pack up all of Deborah's things and put them in the attic." I put my baby in the ground and now all traces of her in the attic? I can't stand it. For now I need everything to stay here.

April 13, 1963

I want to move home. This isn't home anymore.

August 28, 1963

We went to the cemetery. I just cried and cried. C. tried to console me, but I wanted no consolation.

Christmas, 1963

We put up a small tree. I cried to think of how Deborah loved those lights. C. hung our ornament from the first year we were married. I wish I never had made it. I went to Mass alone.

This is as far as we went on my second visit. Char's voice said more than any words; she still felt the pain and sadness of her daughter's death. For some reason I asked her if she remembered John Kennedy being shot. Very quietly she said, "Not really. I was still at Deborah's funeral." And, then, as if to reassure me she said, "I think we're through the worst now."

The third visit I had with Char, she was very perky. She said,

Who Will Value My Tears? – Charlene

"Now I'll tell you a few things about getting over the death of a child. You don't. You change. The world goes on. But there is always just a hint of sadness close by. But at some point you realize you go on, too. It wasn't until 1967 that I even wanted to think about my own life. It took me another year to do anything about it."

January 2, 1967

C. told me he had another job offer. I said, "Take it. Take what you want. You always do." We fought for two hours. All the hurt buried with Deborah came out. I didn't know we could be that ugly! But, once the fight started it wasn't going to stop. We blamed each other for everything. EVERYTHING! Finally I grabbed his arm, and I thought I would hit him. But we both just cried and cried, holding each other on the kitchen floor. I think what was best was we didn't apologize to each other. I, at least, wasn't sorry.

Finally everything that I had held inside came out all over the place.

March 16, 1967

I'm glad we decided to stay here. I'm not ready to move again. Betty [their neighbor] asked me to join a discussion group of women on Thursdays. I told her I had nothing to say. She said, "Then just come listen." C. said now nobody knows where they belong anymore. Everything seems so jumbled up. I realized that I have spent the time since Deborah's death trapped inside myself. I hardly know what is going on in the world. Maybe I'll go to Betty's some week.

With Those Who Grieve

∞

May 15, 1967

Something is happening with women, and it's exciting! The first time I went to Betty's I went all dressed up. These other gals were lounging all over in jeans and talking a different language from me. But they still welcomed me. I was glad a young woman, Sarah, asked, "Who invited Grandma?" It hurt, but then I knew they welcomed me and we all laughed. Laughter! I haven't laughed in years.

July 10, 1967

Clare wants to go to the Grand Canyon; I want to stay and protest. But I'll go on the trip to the Grand Canyon.

August 15, 1967

I'm glad I went with C. We needed to spend that time together again. At the Grand Canyon we appreciated the beauty of life again. I didn't feel that close to God in a long time. When we came home, we packed up all of Deborah's things together except one box, and gave everything to Goodwill. It was hard, but time.

September 14, 1967

Clare and I are arguing again. But about politics, the war, and women's rights. I find it more exciting with the women, but I'm glad our fights at home have changed.

November 3, 1967

Sarah [a member of the women's group] asked me, "What are you going to do with your life?" I have no idea.

Who Will Value My Tears? – Charlene

Christmas, 1967
There is still a hint of sadness, but this year we could celebrate being together again. Nice.

January 1, 1968
My New Year's resolution is to figure out what I am going to do with my life.

At this point, Char and I took a lunch break. I had planned on going home, but we talked for several hours about her involvement with the group of neighborhood women. "Maybe that was when I really started to face Deborah's death. It was my support group, in a way. While others had not lost children, they listened over and over to my pain and sadness. And they invited me into other realms of life. They saw what I could not; that there could still be so much more for me in life. And were they patient! I needed some gentle caring and I found it there. I think I might have been an old, shriveled-up witch the rest of my life. I would have just lived Deborah's death over and over again. Now I had a chance again to find some way to be supported in finding my road back to life." Char's eyes sparkled as she talked.

March 12, 1968
Now I'm the one with the job offer. The college offered me a teaching position in art to fill in for someone until next fall. I'm scared. I'm excited. C. is supportive, but wants to know who will take care of the house, etc. He did not seem overjoyed by my answer, "We will!" My Thursday group can't wait for me to get started. Sarah told me if Grandma Moses did what she did, there's still time for me! They all gave me a beautiful set of paints,

173

and then told me they all expected paintings for Christmas gifts.

May 6, 1968

Married almost ten years . . . do days just drift into one another? So much is just cleaning, cooking, going to the grocery store, getting up, going to bed. We don't seem to really want to spend time with each other much. We have our own exciting worlds without each other.

June 1, 1968

I love being on campus. Sometimes I want to stay longer, but I know C. will be home for dinner. At least conversation isn't boring. But sometimes, with him coming home from the corporate world and me from the college world, discussions move into arguments.

August 31, 1968

The college asked me to teach one class this fall. Thank goodness! C. and I used to enjoy our differences. Now we seem to make everything a fight. When the Chicago Convention happened, he just said, "Now are you proud to be a Democrat?"

October 13, 1968

Clare gave me two wrapped gifts. One was a box of assorted buttons. Inside was a note that said, "I miss being called Buttons." The other was a necklace with a peace symbol. No note. Maybe we can feel joined again.

November 15, 1968

I took in the box of Deborah's things to my art class. I told my students about Deborah and had them do sketches of her things. I wept after class when one student said, "My sister was killed by a car when I was five. Until today I didn't know how to start getting past that." She gave me a beautiful small sketch with rays of sunlight beaming down on some of Deborah's toys. We went out for coffee and cried together about our losses. I had thought I was past my hurt and tears, but they were as fresh as ever.

Christmas, 1968

We hung our ornament on the tree. I had framed the sketch my student did, and gave it to Buttons. At first he just glared at me. Then I told him the story of the sketch, and we sat together crying most of the night by a fire. It was a healing Christmas. C. said he wasn't ready to put it up, but asked if we could wrap it carefully and take it out every Christmas. I was moved. He said, "We need to acknowledge her life as special, not just think about her death."

We ended our visit here for the day. Inside I felt touched by some lingering sadness of my own and also felt I had now been brought into Char's life in an ineffable way. There is something in the telling of stories of loss that somehow binds us together in sadness, hope, healing, and, for me, an intimacy beyond my comprehension. The dynamics are both wrenching and profoundly touching. All pretense is stripped away. Maybe it is one of the few ways we are truly, wonderfully human together. We grope for meaning in meaningless death and somehow find a new shared life. This is why, despite tears and sadness, I feel compelled to do grief work. It is why I tell people I have the best job in the world.

When I next visited Char, I was surprised at the woman who opened the door. She looked ten years younger, had a vibrancy I had not seen, and was dressed in brightly colored clothing. It was like she had come out of mourning. From that day on, our visits would be more casual. I felt free to take off my shoes and put my feet up on her furniture. She and I laughed together. There had been a mutual healing at our last visit. At the time, it seemed nearly unbelievable. But I see this sort of "turning point toward life" frequently in my work. This time, however, I also saw the healing within myself.

That day, just as we had changed, so, too, had the journal that Char showed me. It had few words. It was musty from having been in a flood, but the pages still held treasures. During the next four years of their life together, C. changed jobs three times. Each time they moved to a new area of the country.

"Those four years were full of turmoil in our country," Char said, "and I think I was facing internal turmoil. I missed teaching and being on campus. I missed art. I couldn't seem to find the words to capture my feelings, so I bought this art journal and kept my history through sketches and a few mementos."

We sat together for three hours as she explained the drawings of this period of her life. I felt like I was "meeting" people she had written about. A few of the sketches included various portraits of Clare, from distinguished businessman, to gardener, to a thoughtful pose of a man smoking a pipe and reading intently, to a cartoon of him on the 18th hole of a golf course. There were self-portraits done in pencil, ink, and pastels usually showing a woman who was pensive. I "met" relatives from family gatherings, some of them rendered in cartoon style. There were sketches of the women who had supported her, like Betty and Sarah. Some of the pictures were bleak; many spoke to me of hope. There were a few pictures of Tex.

And then there were drawings (some of them uncompleted) of

Deborah. All of them seemed to have a reverence about them, even the one of her playing. The most striking drawing for me was one of Deborah surrounded by loving drawings of Clare and Char. There were also a few pressed flower petals, some theatre tickets, and small pieces of paper that were obviously private to Char.

Most of the drawings were of people. There were a few of animals and flowers, and one of each of the three homes they had lived in. But it was obvious that people were what mattered to Char.

After we looked through the journal, Char took me to a small room. There on the wall was the sketch her art student had done for her of Deborah's things, a sketch she had done of Clare, and the self-portrait she had given him for their first Christmas. I stood a long time in silence with Char. Finally she said, "How about some lunch?" We never spoke again of her drawings. Perhaps there was no need.

Char began writing again in 1973. They had moved for what would be their last time, and settled in the home she now lives in.

February 1, 1973
Whenever the calendar changes to February, I start thinking about Deborah. I found out about a parents' grief group. C. doesn't want to go, but I think I may. It just feels like there is a freer way to live, and I haven't found it on my own.

April 7, 1973
I went to the grief group. At the last minute C. came along. It's painful, but freeing. I don't think I realized how guilty I've felt for outliving Deborah.

May 23, 1973
I'm just beginning to call this home. I don't trust that we'll be

here, because our last two moves were supposed to be our last. Clare says he's too old (and too important!) to be transferred again. I need roots.

July 4, 1973

A family reunion. I usually hate reunions, but this time I realized that we have all come a long way together. I won't see a lot of these people again. In some cases, thank goodness! But in other cases, I think I feel more of a need to feel close to these people since Deborah's death. Somehow people have become more precious. I take much less for granted.

August 16, 1973

Fifteen years of marriage! Now we're just comfortable old sweaters and shoes to each other. I like that.

September 14, 1973

C. and I are taking a class in gardening together. It has been one of the first things we've really done together with enthusiasm in a while. We are planning which trees and flowers to plant with our new home—I feel we have roots again.

October 17, 1973

Sarah would laugh. I agreed with three other women to display some of my paintings at the library. Maybe my time with art away from words helped clean me out for artistic expression. Maybe.

Thanksgiving, 1973

It was time for a family holiday again at our home. What a family! Ruth does not look well, but surprised me in the kitchen by telling me she knew from the day she met me I was right for Clare. Does it have to take this many years to say these things to each other?

December 12, 1973
Ruth died this morning from some blood disease. How did none of us know? Did we want to know? I feel like I just start to heal from one death, and along comes another. And I know now that they will be happening more and more. C. buries his grief deep inside. I don't know what to say or how to really comfort him.

Christmas, 1973
It's a low-key holiday this year. I decided to buy a live tree to plant in our yard for Ruth. Then I wondered why I never had done something like that for Deborah. So, I bought two trees we can plant in spring.

New Year's Day, 1974
I don't know how to start a new year. No plans. No resolutions.

January 26, 1974
I started to see a counselor to get over Deborah's death. I need to try to find a way to live with these waves of great sadness and depression.

February 5, 1974
C. and I talked about going to counseling together. He said his work is how he heals. But it seems he works more and heals less.

With Those Who Grieve

∞

February 17, 1974

Jane [a counselor] suggested I go visit Deborah's grave on what would have been her eleventh birthday. We've visited the grave a few times a year, but never in March. I think it's time.

March 2, 1974

Clare and I have made plans to go to Deborah's grave. I went through the box of things today that we've kept all these years, and decided to leave her baby blanket at her grave. She wouldn't be a baby now. I need to admit that to myself.

March 11, 1974

It was painful going to Deborah's grave and seeing the small lamb headstone. But I realized that it is weatherworn. Rather like me inside. I held on to her blanket for what seemed like forever. Then C. and I placed it softly across her grave. Tears for both of us, but a freedom in feeling she and we are truly at rest. I don't expect myself to never cry, or never feel robbed, or never feel angry again over her death, but I think it will now be subdued. I feel closure.

March 14, 1974

We planted the trees for Deborah and Ruth. I feel serene.

April 3, 1974

I need to go away with C. To see who we've become these past few years.

May 11, 1974

A week on the ocean. No phones. No bills. Just relax and be together. Clare said he thought he'd have trouble not working, but he's having a great time. Such simple pleasures like leisurely meals together, leisurely evenings together, walking hand in hand in silence. It's good to live simply again.

July 15, 1974
The local college offered me a full-time teaching job. I feel like I've been away from the world for so long, yet my art has kept me alive. C.'s pleased for me. We just seem to get more and more supportive of each other.

August 16, 1974
Sixteen years together. We have an ebb and flow; a separateness and togetherness.

Since Clare has taken up golf again, I got him a set of clubs. I did NOT expect a set, too, but it may be fun to learn with him.

October 15, 1974
It is GREAT to be teaching again. This time I have some more "free form" classes and it's exciting to watch what students do. I get a lot of inspiration from them.

Christmas, 1974
We invited our families to our home for Christmas dinner. It felt great to have the kids running around and making noise. I didn't realize how much I missed watching them grow up while we were moving around.

January 3, 1975
C. had to be rushed to the hospital. Maybe a mild heart attack. It was frightening to realize I could lose him that fast. But I think

With Those Who Grieve

∞

I'm strong enough within myself now to go on alone.

February 18, 1975
I hired a nurse for C. He's insulted I won't quit work, but it keeps me going and feeling stimulated. His doctor wants him to rest two more weeks before going back to work. Ha!

March 19, 1975
Clare is back at work. I didn't feel so sad this year about Deborah. I've said my goodbye.

May 3, 1975
I tried to get Clare to golf, but he still is apprehensive about his heart. His doctors say he's doing well, but he doesn't seem to believe it. He has taken up gardening again, which calms his nerves AND mine.

August 7, 1975
We went to a golf outing for Clare's business. It was good to have him feel comfortable being out again.

October 31, 1975
Clare is back to his good humor. We went to a Halloween party dressed in clothes from the 50s. I'm not sure some of his junior execs understood.

We had a great time, which surprised me since C. seems to enjoy only those parties he hosts.

Thanksgiving, 1975
We fought all day. I didn't realize until nighttime that C. was

depressed over Ruth's death. On campus, I just get more and more into life.

Christmas, 1975
Dinner with Clare's dad. They both sat around being depressed. I may give up holidays for next year.

February 1, 1976
At the last minute, the school asked me if I would oversee some kind of artistic extravaganza for the Bicentennial. There's almost no budget, so I'll have to give creative assignments to my students.

May 14, 1976
One class of mine took a whole cement wall near the gymnasium and painted it with terrific flags, symbolizing what they liked about the USA. We were asked to paint over it. I was mad!! But then the local news picked it up, and now the school "Is proud of its Fine Arts department." Part of me is still mad, but Clare says just accept the good news.

May 18, 1976
I'm so used to Clare being in the press and going to awards dinners for him. But now with this flag painting, newspapers are calling and asking for interviews with me. I feel like I have something to say, but feel awkward. I think I'm an introverted artist more comfortable without any spotlight.

July 4, 1976
The "flag wall" is still making news. I am proud of my students,

but feel that the coverage is too much now. Clare encourages me to have a sense of humor, and to remember to use this as a bargaining chip for a raise. He's probably realistic, but I feel it is all taking away from the artistic.

August 16, 1976

Clare took me out to a little wooded area near the school. As we walked through the woods we talked about our marriage, our past, our future. It was a simply beautiful way to spend our anniversary. Then, I couldn't believe it: Like a tiny cottage in a story, a small new wooden building with lots of glass stood before us! Clare had been working on a studio for me since March. It is the greatest anniversary gift ever!

The walls were bare except for the self-portrait I gave him our first Christmas and the student drawing of Deborah's things. I didn't know what to say. . . . Clare said that was HIS best gift from me!

Sometimes I get bored with marriage or tired of rubbing up against C. every day, and then something like this moment happens and I know I wouldn't choose to repeat my life. It is full as it is.

Char and I took a break for the day here. She told me all about her studio, and all of the good and rich times she spent there. "Usually I spent time alone there. It gave me time to be reflective, to think about my life, to think about a lot . . . art, my marriage, and God. I felt I could paint more slowly and more inspired there alone.

"One day I was very angry at Clarence. I went and spent the day and the night there. The next morning I realized that while my studio could give me respite and be like a retreat for me, I didn't feel

right using it as a place to hide from Clare. I never spent the night there again."

The next visit Char looked tired. She told me she had been up most of the night with her journals. I said we could meet another time. She insisted we meet then. I think we both knew we were headed for the story of the end of Clarence's life.

February 4, 1977

Clare has been talking a lot about death lately. He wants to make sure that I know where all the papers are, where the banking accounts are, and most difficult for me, where he wants to be buried. We talked about being buried closer to where we live now, but I guess deep in our hearts we both know we want to be buried by Deborah. Long ago when I married a man ten years older than I am, I thought I was lucky to have someone who "knew the way" through life. But now Clare reminds me almost daily that he is almost sixty. As if that is a death sentence.

April 1, 1977

Spring seems to have brought Clare out of his depression about death. He's counting the days until the golf club opens.

May 13, 1977

After many long talks, Clare wants to convert to Catholicism. I kidded him that he'd be ruining a whole topic for family gatherings. But inside I don't know why he'd want to convert at this point. He just says, "It will make everything easier," but I argued that we had done fine with our individual faiths. "I want a shared faith," he said adamantly. "We have one," I yelled, not quite knowing what I meant. I think I feel what we've shared has bond-ed us in a faith of each other because of God. I'm too tired to be a theologian.

June 15, 1977
Clare and I are planning a vacation to the mountains. We both need it.

July 2, 1977
We arrived at Hazel and Burt's [business friends] cabin today. It's simple and serene. We hiked among wild flowers, and I picked C. a bouquet. We sat in comfortable silence by the fire most of the night.

July 10, 1977
Even though my studio gives me a chance to observe nature closely, it's nice to enjoy different wildlife on leisurely walks together. We've both slowed down in a wonderful way. We know we'll be there for each other, and I don't think we expect much more of each other. It does take a long time to get here!

September 24, 1977
It's great to be back at school! I think I'm becoming used to seasons and cycles of life, and feel better when each one comes. I'm experimenting with a lot of art media; the students stimulate me.

October 15, 1977
Since C. converted, his religious zeal is almost too much for me. He spends less time at work, but then spends half of his nights at the parish. Maybe it will wear off a bit. It's like he's making up for lost centuries! And, I thought it would mean LESS argu-

ments; now we argue over the Church's stance on about EVERY-THING. The other day I told him I had had enough—I was going to become a Presbyterian!

Thanksgiving, 1977
It was sad and joyous to have the family together. The kids aren't kids anymore. Fewer places are needed at the table because people have moved, or gone their own ways, or died. I realized Deborah would be a young woman now; a teenager. Now I'm the one depressed about aging. How do we become old so fast?

Christmas, 1977
We entertained the families of Clare's business this afternoon—no way to spend Christmas! I'm exhausted.

January 2, 1978
Clare took down the tree. Before he put everything away, he asked me into the den to see the tree. All that was left hanging was that weary ornament I made for our first Christmas. Clare pointed to it and said, "THAT is why we have stayed together so well." I thought he was joking. He became very tender, but very serious. "We have been content with what we've had. That's the secret."

February 6, 1978
I swear if election were by popular vote, Clare would be pope tomorrow!

March 28, 1978
The winter is long. I have been bitten by Deborah remembrances again.

With Those Who Grieve

April 15, 1978

Income tax day. Why don't they just charge a one-time tax the day you're born? And April means the golf club is open again. Maybe I'll take up golf again. If Clare isn't on the course, he's at church. Or on the course with Father Tim. Maybe they could put up a parish on the 19th hole!

May 1, 1978

This semester has been the least invigorating. So many students think bleak art is profound. Most of it is just sloppy. Thank goodness for my studio!

May 12, 1978

It's been fun getting out golfing with Clare a few times. We both laugh at my game, but it's great to get outdoors and put all my thoughts in that little ball getting to the flag. MaryBeth [a coworker] wants me to join a women's league with her. I may do it just for the fun.

May 29, 1978

Don [a friend] and Father Tim came to my door. Clare's dead. Clare's dead. My God in heaven, Clare's dead.

May 30, 1978

MaryBeth came over and spent the day answering the phone. She offered to stay the night. I want Clare. I can't make decisions. He isn't dead to me yet.

May 31, 1978

Father Tim stopped by to help plan the funeral Mass. I was furious that Clare had left funeral plans with Father Tim, but not me. I say things I don't believe, like telling the funeral home Clare had no suits, and to bury him in his golf clothes with a rosary. I can't eat. I sleep and wake up with my arm over his empty side of the bed. MaryBeth seems to be running everything. I want to yell, "Stop!" But I know I can't do it all alone, either. I laugh when things aren't funny. I barely cry.

June 1, 1978
The wake. So many people. So many hugs. So many tears. So many words I can't remember. I feel like I'm watching an awful movie. "You're so brave," someone said to me. How odd.

June 15, 1978
The funeral Mass. The trek to the cemetery. I wanted to yell at Clare at the cemetery, "You're at peace. Deborah's at peace. BUT WHERE AM I?" And where is that loving God?

July 3, 1978
Friends invited me out on their boat for the 4th. I don't feel like celebrating. Anything.

August 29, 1978
I decided to invite a few friends over for a Labor Day picnic. Instead of having Marge clean the house, I decided to do it myself. I realized that Clare died three months ago when I started to clean off his bureau to dust under his comb and wallet and a small pile of change. I held a few of the coins in my hands, then let them slide through my fingers to the floor. And then I threw myself on the bed and cried harder than I ever have in my life.

Am I only meant to love and lose? Deborah's death was awful, but little by little I could let out my grief, finally, with Clare. But without Clare, who will value my tears?

Labor Day, 1978
It rained all day. I got mad at everyone and everything! I felt angry at friends who still had their mates. I felt angry at the reminder of those who don't. I'm mad at a God who takes away everyone I love. I'm mad at the rain.

September 15, 1978
I mixed too many tranquilizers and alcohol. How did MaryBeth know something was wrong just because I didn't answer the phone? I kept telling the doctors it was an accident, but I remember being angry I wasn't dead. I had to stay for forty-eight hours, and now I'm stuck with MaryBeth as a baby-sitter.

September 27, 1978
I had a horrible fight with MaryBeth, and yet there was something so wonderful about knowing I could yell at her without her leaving. I can't even remember what triggered it, but I remember throwing a plate of spaghetti at her. It missed her, hit the wall, and flew all over. The plate broke, and it felt WONDERFUL. I threw a water goblet at the wall and it shattered. I remember yelling, "You want to know how I feel? You want to? I feel like that!" And I pointed at the wall. I went to the cupboard and found a half dozen saucers and destroyed them. The sound was wonderful. I felt muscles loosen that have held in everything for four months.

MaryBeth wanted to clean up the mess, but I wouldn't let

her. "Leave it alone! I'm an artist. That's my masterpiece to death!"

October 2, 1978
MaryBeth leaves tomorrow. I'll miss her, but I think I'll be all right alone. She keeps insisting she could stay another week. And then what? Another week? No, it is time to face that I must now live solo, but hopefully not alone.

October 3, 1978
Goodbye, MaryBeth. Goodbye. All the goodbyes. It's hard to want to say hello again.

This was the last entry Char made. Beginning New Year's Day, 1979, she kept a brief accounting of her new life without Clare.

She says it took nearly five years for her to visit the graves of Clare and Deborah. "I realized that when I drove out of the cemetery, that one day a hearse would be driving me into that same cemetery. Somehow I just knew it was time to get on with my life. And to find my masterpiece to life."

For Further Reading

Death and Grief

Becker, Ernest. *The Denial of Death*. New York: The Free Press, 1973.

Kastenbaum, Robert and Aisenberg, Ruth. *The Psychology of Death*. New York: Springer Publishing, 1972.

Kübler-Ross, Elisabeth. *On Death and Dying*. New York: Macmillan, 1969.

Kübler-Ross, Elisabeth. *Questions and Answers on Death and Dying*. New York: Collier Macmillan, 1974.

Parkes, Colin Murray. *Bereavement*. New York: Penguin, 1972.

Tatelbaum, Judy. *The Courage to Grieve*. New York: Harper & Row, 1980.

Wangerin, Walter. *Mourning into Dancing*. Grand Rapids, Michigan: Zondervan, 1992.

Westberg, Granger E. *Good Grief.* Philadelphia: Fortress Press, 1971.

Children and Grief

Brown, M.W. *The Dead Bird.* New York: Dell Publishing Company, Inc., 1979.

Grollman, Earl A., ed. *Explaining Death to Children*. Boston: Beacon Press, 1967.

Huntley, Theresa. *Helping Children Grieve*. Minneapolis: Augsburg Fortress, 1991.

Death of a Child

Bordow, Joan. *The Ultimate Loss: Coping with the Death of a Child.* New York: Beaufort Books, 1982.

Storkey, Elaine. *Losing a Child*. Elgin, Illinois: Lion Publishing, 1990.

Strommen, Merton and A. Irene. *Five Cries of Grief.* San Francisco: HarperCollins, 1993.

The Compassionate Friends is an organization dedicated to developing resources that address coping with the grief of losing a child. It publishes resources for parents, siblings, stepparents, grandparents, friends, and others who provide support and assistance in the grieving process. Their national office address is: The Compassionate Friends, P.O. Box 3696, Oak Brook, IL 60522-3696.

Suicide

Chilstrom, Corinne. *Andrew, You Died Too Soon: A Family Experience of Grieving and Living Again.* Minneapolis: Augsburg Fortress, 1993.

Hewett, John J. *After Suicide.* Wayne Oates, ed. Philadelphia: Westminster Press, 1980.

Shneidman, Edwin. *Definition of Suicide.* New York: John Wiley & Sons, 1985.

Death of a Spouse

Caine, Lynn. *Widow.* New York: William Morrow & Co., 1974.

Lewis, C. S. *A Grief Observed.* New York: Seabury Press, 1963.

Death of a Parent

Myers, Edward. *When Parents Die: A Guide for Adults.* New York: Viking Penguin, 1986.

Inspirational/Theological

Keller, Paul F. *Living the Promises of God: 365 Readings for Recovery from Grief or Loss.* Minneapolis: Augsburg Fortress, 1988.

Marty, Martin E. *A Cry of Absence: Reflections for the Winter of the Heart.* San Francisco: Harper & Row, 1985.

Nygaard, Reuel and Doud, Guy. *Tragedy to Triumph.* Elgin, Illinois: LifeJourney Books, 1994.

Rosenthal, Ted. *How Could I Not Be Among You?* New York: Brazilier, 1973.

Simundson, Daniel J. *Where Is God in My Suffering?* Minneapolis: Augsburg Fortress, 1983.

Springteen, Anne. *Handful of Thorns: Poems of Grief.* Valparaiso, Indiana: Orchard House, 1977.

For Further Reading

∞

For Caregivers and Professionals

Bocckelman, Wilfred. *Finding the Right Words: Offering Care and Comfort When You Don't Know What to Say.* Minneapolis: Augsburg Fortress, 1990.

Garfield, Charles A. *Psychosocial Care of the Dying Patient.* New York: McGraw-Hill, 1978.

Worden, William J. *Grief Counseling and Grief Therapy.* New York: Springer Publishing Company, 1982.

LIVING THROUGH GRIEF

Sooner or later grief comes to everyone. We do not fully understand it until we walk through it ourselves. But grief has a common pattern, and it helps if we know what to expect.

This book explains the stages of grief and suggests practical steps for learning to live again.

It shares the special comfort and resources the Christian faith offers.

It points the way to healing and hope.

You can find this and other Lion Pocketbooks at your local bookstore.

Living Through Grief $2.99
Harold Bauman   ISBN 0-7459-1617-1

LION
PUBLISHING

LOSING A CHILD

The loss of a child may happen in many different ways. But each lost child is precious. And behind each loss there is grief. How can we cope with the shock and the pain?

Where can we turn for help?

Who will answer the 'whys' and 'if onlys'?

This is a helpful, positive book. It faces the pain; it also offers encouragement and hope.

You can find this and other Lion Pocketbooks at your local bookstore.

Losing A Child $2.99
Elaine Storkey   ISBN 0-7459-1842-5

LION
PUBLISHING

WHAT HAPPENS AFTER DEATH?

There are only two certainties for any person:
one is birth, the other is death.

And while one is greeted with celebration, the
other is shrouded in mystery.

This small Pocketbook explores the Bible's
answers to humanity's questions surrounding
life after death.

You can find this and other Lion Pocketbooks
at your local bookstore.

What Happens After Death $2.99
David Winter   ISBN 0-7459-2137-X

LION
PUBLISHING